Praise for

NAKED FINANCE

"This is a highly recommended book: straightforward, easy to read, very clear concepts and content and very well explained."
Business Executive

"An excellent Return on Investment! Covers the fundamentals and basic principles of finance in a clear and simplified way. Essential reading for the successful manager."
Robert King, Group HR Manager, Harvey Nichols

"Nobody makes this subject more interesting and enjoyable to understand. If you want to be credible in any business conversation this book is an essential tool. You can try and pretend that understanding finance is not important to you, but actually it is essential in any business role. If you don't know your asset turnover from your cash flow, read this now!"
Fraser Longden, Director of Retail HR, B & Q

"Naked Finance combines many aspects that are not seen in books that introduce finance to managers. It is written by an outstanding practitioner, it has a high degree of sophistication which will not be perceived by the technically untrained reader, it outlines how managers can understand and use finance in their jobs, and it explains it all in a clear, witty and informative manner. It is a practical and reliable guide for managers in any type of business. All in all it is a stunning introduction to finance which should be part of every manager's toolkit."
John Smullen, Senior Academic Advisor, University of Greenwich

NAKED FINANCE

Business finance pure and simple

DAVID MECKIN

NICHOLAS BREALEY
PUBLISHING

LONDON · BOSTON

To Shaaron, Kieran and Sinéad

First published by
Nicholas Brealey Publishing in 2007
Reprinted 2008, 2009 (twice)

3-5 Spafield Street
Clerkenwell, London
EC1R 4QB, UK
Tel: +44 (0)20 7239 0360
Fax: +44 (0)20 7239 0370

20 Park Plaza, Suite 1115A
Boston
MA 02116, USA
Tel: (888) BREALEY
Fax: (617) 523 3708

www.nicholasbrealey.com
www.www.insight-financial.com

ISBN: 978-1-85788-394-7

Library of Congress Cataloging-in-Publication Data

Meckin, David.
  Naked finance : business finance pure and simple / David Meckin.
    p. cm.
  Includes index.
  1. Business enterprises--Finance. 2. Financial statements. 3. Business
mathematics. I. Title.
  HG4026.M433 2007
  658.15--dc22

2007021556

British Library Cataloguing in Publication Data
A catalogue record for this book is available from the
British Library.

Images © 2007 Jupiterimages Corporation.

Printed in Finland by WS Bookwell.

Contents

1 WHAT IS NAKED FINANCE?

You've just arrived at work at half past eight in the morning. Your planner suggests another day of emails, telephone calls, meetings, writing reports, and, if you're lucky, maybe a rushed sandwich and a coffee squeezed somewhere in between. The fact that two members of your team are off sick and you are still trying to fill an opening for an assistant doesn't worry you. That's just another day at the office!

However, you are concerned because sales in your division are below plan and you're under pressure to reduce costs. To help manage these issues the finance division provides regular reports, but you can't make any sense out of them. Matters aren't helped by the fact that the computer equipment used in your department is out of date and you need to put forward a commercial case for replacing it. Stress levels are further increasing because next week you have to present your budget proposals for the forthcoming year. As if to add insult to injury, the company's share price has been falling over the past few weeks and there are rumors of staff cutbacks – your team wants to know what's going on.

The normal day-to-day demands of the job are well within your management capabilities. It's these financial issues that give you a headache. Nobody has ever explained how to balance sales against costs, how to interpret financial reports, how to argue a case for new computer equipment, or how to prepare a budget. You also have no idea why your company's stock value keeps falling and you certainly don't understand why staff layoffs should result. In fact, this whole finance thing is a mystery to you. What you need is a book that explains all of these concepts in simple, easy-to-understand terms. Indeed, a visit to the local bookstore seems like time well invested.

In the bookstore it doesn't take long to track down the finance section. The array of books is vast. Your finger moves along the shelf. The titles alone are offputting. *Management Accounting in the Corporate Environment, An Introduction to Company Valuation Methodologies*, and *The Ultimate Dictionary for Financial Professionals* just don't seem to be what you're looking for. In fact, when you reach a text called *Linear Regression Techniques for the Modern Financial Manager*, you're about ready to give up.

All you want is a book that explains financial principles in easy-to-understand terms and demonstrates how these can be practically applied in your day-to-day job. This is what *Naked Finance* is all about. By stripping business finance down to its pure and simple basics, the intention is to provide a clear, unimpeded view of the world of financial management and how it works. **The objective of this book is to provide managers with all the financial skills they will ever need, in straightforward, non-technical terms.**

Why do managers need to understand finance?

Financial management permeates every aspect of business. As you progress through this book, it will become evident that financial management is not a topic that is simply 'nice to know', it is an essential skill for most managers. So it might be useful if we clarified at the outset what we mean by the term 'financial management.'

The word finance is commonly defined as 'pertaining to money.' It follows that financial management involves the management of money. However, financial management within a business environment means more than this – there are usually very clear objectives. Consequently, it is essential that the decisions you make as a manager are consistent with these objectives. In order to do this, you need to develop certain skills.

If you ask most managers how much of their working lives they spend making financial decisions, they will probably say very little.

They therefore mistakenly assume that understanding financial management is not particularly important. Indeed, many managers regard business operations and financial management as totally separate disciplines. It is sometimes intimated that accountants spend most of their time preparing and analyzing reams of figures, while the management team get on with the main task of running the business.

Several miles apart

Business   Finance

THE PERCEIVED RELATIONSHIP BETWEEN BUSINESS AND FINANCE

In reality, business management and finance are intrinsically linked, with many managerial decisions having a direct impact on financial performance. Launching new products, offering credit to customers, negotiating terms with suppliers, employing staff, purchasing equipment, and even ordering stationery can affect financial performance.

The bare bones
A key element in making a sound management decision is to understand how it will affect financial performance.

How is this book going to help me?

That's a very good question! You're only into the first few pages and you're already beginning to think financially. When you buy this book you are making an investment – you are not only investing cash, but you are also (hopefully) going to invest time reading it. It is hardly surprising, then, that you're going to want a return on this investment. People invest time and money in businesses in the hope of obtaining some sort of return on their investment. If they don't anticipate a return, they are not going to invest.

We are about to remove the mystique that surrounds the topic of business finance and show that it is really quite straightforward and (most importantly) relevant. In the world of financial management, there is one tenet that is central to success:

Keep it simple!

Developing an understanding of financial management is very similar to learning to drive a car. You don't need to understand the technicalities of the internal combustion engine in order to be a successful driver. In order to drive a car, all you need are three skill sets:

* **You need to know where you are going**
* **You need to understand the information around you**
* **You need to control where you are going**

Financial management demands the same three skill sets.

If you're planning a car journey you need to decide where you want to go and how you're going to get there. This process can be greatly simplified by breaking the journey down into stages. Not surprisingly, in business people follow the same approach. At the outset, financial objectives have to be identified. As you will discover, one commonly quoted goal is a profit target, how much money the business wants to make. How it will achieve this can be determined by breaking down the profit-making process into several distinct stages.

Once you're in the car and on your way, there is lots of information available to aid your progress. This information is gathered from two distinct sources. There is information inside the car, such as that presented on the dashboard, which tells you how you are currently progressing. There is also information outside the car, such as that presented on road signs, which tells you what to expect ahead. Business is no different. Information is vital to achieving commercial goals. The business equivalent of a dashboard is a set of financial statements. At the end of every trading period, businesses commonly produce financial statements summarizing their trading activities. This is very useful for assessing current performance. To further assist management, information is available that is produced outside the business. The business equivalent of road signs is the financial press, which can prove invaluable when assessing future trading prospects.

The third skill set a driver needs is how to operate the various controls such as the accelerator, brake, steering wheel, and so on. Just as controls exist to ensure the vehicle is doing what you want it to, so there are financial controls that can be used to ensure the business is doing what you want it to. In business there are three financial issues that need to be continually monitored and controlled:

* **Profit**
  Controlling profit involves managing sales and costs.
* **Cash flow**
  Cash flow, as we will discover, is very different from profit. Controlling cash flow means ensuring that cash is available to pay bills as they arise.
* **Long-term projects**
  Making profit and managing cash flow are issues that need to be addressed on a day-to-day basis. However, sometimes businesses embark on projects that may have an impact for several years, such as moving into a new head office or investing in new computer equipment. These are long-term projects and, as such, need to be managed in a very specific way.

We have just established that the skill sets needed to manage the finances of a business are much the same as those needed to drive a car. The similarity does not stop there. A car is a machine designed to get people from one point to another. What we are going to be looking at in this book is the financial machine, which is designed to get a business from one point to another. In both instances, there is a starting point, a journey, and a destination.

Financial management comprises three skill sets:

Setting financial objectives	**Using financial information**	**Providing financial control**
You need to know where you are going	You need to understand the information around you	You need to control where you are going

FINANCIAL MANAGEMENT IS LIKE DRIVING A CAR

Stripping it down to basics...

The structure of this book should now make sense. Below is an overview of all the chapters, showing how the three skill sets identified above interrelate.

The starting point: Where do you want to go?

Before embarking on any journey, you need to decide where you want to go. In Chapters 2 to 5 we examine how businesses set financial objectives and outline the processes they need to go through in order to achieve them.

The journey: How are you progressing?

Once you commence the journey, you need to assess your progress. In Chapters 6 to 9 we look at how to use financial information, which is readily available in the business world, in order to assess performance.

The destination: Are you going in the right direction?

Throughout the journey, it is essential that you make sure you are going in the right direction. In Chapters 10 to 17 we examine the techniques that are most commonly used to control the financial performance of a business.

In Chapter 18, the last chapter of the book, we review the various skill sets and show how they can be combined to plan and manage a profitable business.

There are two points you should bear in mind when reading this book:

* **Financial principles are not hard to grasp**
  You may be surprised at just how simple some of the concepts are.
* **Financial principles can help you make better managerial decisions**
  If you understand financial principles, you will have a far greater appreciation of the financial implications of the managerial decisions you make.

A note on currency

Throughout this book all monetary amounts are quoted in dollars, but you shouldn't conclude from this that we are about to look at financial management as it applies in North America. This book is about financial principles, which are the same whether you live in North America, South America, Europe, Africa, Asia, Australasia, or even Antarctica! We have adopted the dollar sign simply because it is a readily recognized currency symbol throughout the world.

A note on terminology

The world of finance is littered with jargon and the precise terms used can vary not just between countries, but also between businesses within those countries. Consequently, expressions may be used in this book that differ from those you tend to encounter. Don't let this distract you. The point to note is, regardless of the terminology used, the concepts are always the same, and making sense of these principles will help you be successful.

Part One

SETTING FINANCIAL OBJECTIVES

To manage the finances of a business

you need to know where you are going

2 IS IT ALL ABOUT PROFIT?

Every day managers are bombarded by numbers: sales, margins, salaries, stock levels, profit, cash, and share prices – the list is endless. The situation is not helped by the fact that the mantra from on high regularly changes from 'increase sales' to 'cut costs,' 'reduce stock levels,' 'improve cash flow,' 'cut staff,' or 'increase profit.' If only people would make up their minds! How can you be expected to make sound managerial decisions when you're not given clear guidance about what the business is trying to achieve?

You will be relieved to hear that the primary financial objective of most businesses rarely changes. What does change is how they try to achieve that objective. Once you understand what the goal is, the various methods available for attaining that goal will make a lot more sense. **In this chapter we going to look at the role of profit in business and also introduce another concept regularly talked about, cash flow.**

What does a business need to survive?

Business is all about trade, and trade can be defined as 'the activities of buying and selling.' Since buying activities involve expenditure while selling activities involve revenue, it follows that any entity concerned with the management of revenue and expenditure can be regarded as a business.

Whatever your business, how can you ensure it will survive? Unfortunately, many businesses close down within their first year of operation. This is not necessarily because their products are of poor quality or their customer service is lacking. The most common reason is poor financial management. There are two prerequisites for survival: sound management of the business itself and sound management of its finances. If either of these is lacking, the business will have a very short life.

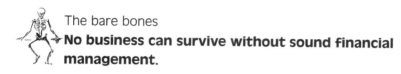

The bare bones
No business can survive without sound financial management.

What is the objective of financial management?

If you want to start up a business, some form of investment will usually be required at the outset. This investment may be provided by you, your friends and relatives, or the public at large. Alternatively, you may resort to borrowing the money.

Having raised the necessary funds, you no doubt want a return on this investment. In other words, you want to start off with a pile of money at the beginning of the year and wind up with a larger pile of money at the end. This increase in the pile of money is known as 'profit,' and making profit is the primary financial objective of most businesses. In essence, profit answers the question, 'How much bigger is the pile of money I end up with, compared to the pile of money I started off with?' What exactly we mean by the term 'pile of money' will be examined later in this chapter.

Not every organization is created with the explicit intention of making a profit, for example government agencies and charities. Even in these cases, though, there is an implied profit target. Government agencies receive revenue from the government and are expected to use this money to provide services. This means that they want to balance their revenue and costs, so they do have a profit target: it just happens to be nil. Charities are often perceived as operating on similar principles, inasmuch as they also want to balance their revenue and costs.

Pile of money at start of year   Pile of money at end of year

THE PROFIT MOTIVE

In fact, some charities like their revenue to exceed their expenditure, so they have funds that can be used to develop the charity in the future. Any excess of revenue over expenditure is often referred to as a 'surplus.'

For simplicity and to avoid repetition, we are going to assume we are dealing with companies for the rest of this book. In other words, we are going to assume we are dealing with businesses that raise funds from shareholders in exchange for shares. Nevertheless, the principles we examine are relevant to all types of business, whether they be sole traders, partnerships, corporations, government agencies, or charities.

To put it simply, the objective of financial management in the majority of businesses is to take a business idea and turn it into profit. It is all very well having a good business idea, but if you are unable to generate profit, you wind up with an idea but no business! Regrettably, there is no magic formula for coming up with an idea that will make you millions of dollars. However, sound financial management significantly increases the likelihood of your business producing a profit at the end of the day.

Business   requires   Financial   to deliver   Profit
idea   management

THE ROLE OF FINANCE IN BUSINESS

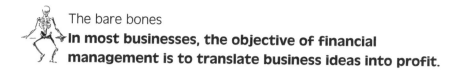

The bare bones
In most businesses, the objective of financial management is to translate business ideas into profit.

What is profit?

Since profit is at the heart of financial management, it is essential to understand the concept. Here's a challenge. Try asking someone, 'How do you calculate profit?' It is very likely the response you get will be something like, 'Profit is sales less costs.' Is this true, though? Suppose you decide to set up your own business selling pens – let's apply this definition.

On 1 January you invest $1,000 of your own money to get the business started and you use this during the month to buy pens. During February you sell all the pens for $1,500. Business does not get much simpler than this! Let's try and establish how much profit you make in each month.

In January you spend $1,000 on pens, but no sales take place. Applying the calculation suggested above ('profit is sales less costs') to that period, we get the following result:

Profit in January   = Sales in January LESS Costs in January
                          = Nil sales LESS $1,000 costs
                          = $1,000 loss

In February no expenditure takes place, but sales of $1,500 are achieved:

Profit in February   = Sales in February LESS Costs in February
                          = $1,500 sales LESS Nil costs
                          = $1,500 profit

These results suggest you made a loss of $1,000 in January, while you made a profit of $1,500 in February. If this is true, this begs a question: What did you do wrong in January to generate a loss? The answer is you bought pens. So what did you do right in February to generate a profit? The answer is you sold pens. This would seem to suggest that if you want your business to be successful in the future, you should stop buying pens and concentrate exclusively on selling them. That is lunacy!

What we have identified is a different concept – cash flow. It is a fact that in January you paid out $1,000 more cash than you received. It is also a fact that in February you received $1,500 more cash than you paid out. The calculation we have been applying so far is that for cash flow.

The bare bones

Cash flow in a period = Cash received in a period
LESS Cash paid out in a period

Profit has got nothing to do with cash flow. The real formula for calculating profit may seem bizarre at first sight, but there is logic behind it:

Profit is calculated by taking sales in a period and deducting the costs incurred to produce that period's sales.

There are a couple of very important subtleties in this statement. First, profit is calculated by examining the sales in a period, regardless of when the cash is received. Second, we deduct the expenditure incurred to produce those sales, regardless of when the cash is paid out.

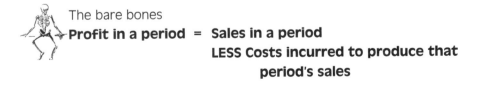

The bare bones

Profit in a period = Sales in a period
LESS Costs incurred to produce that
period's sales

This calculation will make a lot more sense if we apply it to some live figures. Let's return to your pen business. In January no sales take place, so the sales figure in the profit calculation reads zero. According to the profit calculation, if there are no sales, you can't have incurred any costs to produce those sales. This gives us the following result:

Profit in January   = Sales in January
                       LESS Costs incurred to produce January's sales
                     = Nil sales LESS Nil costs
                     = $0

In February you achieve sales of $1,500 by selling stock pur-
chased in the previous month for $1,000. As a result, the sales figure
in the profit calculation reads $1,500 and the cost figure reads $1,000:

Profit in February   = Sales in February
                       LESS Costs incurred to produce February's sales
                     = $1,500 sales LESS $1,000 costs
                     = $500 profit

So profit in January was nil, while profit in February was $500.
This is very different from the cash flow of the business, where there
was a $1,000 outflow in January, compared with a $1,500 inflow in
February. This confirms that profit and cash flow are not the same
thing.

What does profit measure if it doesn't measure cash flow?
Earlier on we noted that the objective of most businesses is to start off
with a pile of money and wind up with a larger pile of money at the
end of the year. We now need to think very carefully about what we
mean by this statement. When we talk about someone having piles of
money, we are not saying they are literally surrounded by huge bun-
dles of cash teetering precariously over their head. We normally mean
they have an expansive house, maybe a few cars, or even a private air-
craft. In other words, we are talking about wealth.

This is what profit measures – profit measures changes in
wealth. When a company states it has made a profit, it is not saying it
has more cash, it is saying its wealth has gone up. In other words, it
owns more. Conversely, when a company makes a loss, its wealth has
gone down – it owns less.

The bare bones
Profit measures changes in wealth.

A **profit** means wealth
has been created

A **loss** means wealth
has been destroyed

UNDERSTANDING PROFIT

Let's confirm that the profit calculation really does measure changes in wealth. In order to do this, we need to know how wealth is calculated:

Wealth = What an individual (or business) owns
LESS What an individual (or business) owes at a specific point in time

Applying this definition to your pen business, let's identify your wealth at the start of January.

CALCULATION OF WEALTH AT START OF JANUARY

	$
What do you own?	
Cash	1,000
What do you owe?	
No debts	0
WEALTH AT START OF JANUARY	1,000

At the start of January, you have $1,000 cash and owe nothing, so your wealth is $1,000. Now let's examine your wealth at the end of January.

CALCULATION OF WEALTH AT END OF JANUARY

	$
What do you own?	
Pens	1,000
What do you owe?	
No debts	0
WEALTH AT END OF JANUARY	1,000

At the end of January you have no cash left, but you do have $1,000 worth of pens. We know this is what the pens are worth because that is what you paid for them. As a result, your wealth during the month is unchanged. There is no profit and no loss, even though sales are nil.

Now let's turn our attention to February. If your wealth is $1,000 at the end of January, it must still be $1,000 at the start of February. However, the situation alters during the next few weeks.

CALCULATION OF WEALTH AT END OF FEBRUARY

	$
What do you own?	
Cash	1,500
What do you owe?	
No debts	0
WEALTH AT END OF FEBRUARY	1,500

At the end of February you have disposed of all your pens, but you do have $1,500 cash. Your wealth has increased by $500, from $1,000 at the start of the month to $1,500 at the end. In other words, you have made a profit of $500. This change in wealth is summarized in the following diagram.

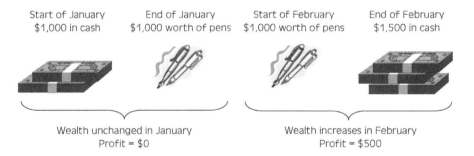

Start of January	End of January	Start of February	End of February
$1,000 in cash	$1,000 worth of pens	$1,000 worth of pens	$1,500 in cash

Wealth unchanged in January
Profit = $0

Wealth increases in February
Profit = $500

PROFIT MEASURES CHANGES IN WEALTH

As you can see, the calculation of profit does indeed measure changes in wealth.

Is cash flow important?

Having established that profit is not the same as cash flow, we now need to understand the relevance of cash flow. We have noted that the sales and cost figures included in the calculation of profit do not necessarily bear any relationship to when cash is received or paid out. This is evident when looking at the first month's operation of your pen business. In January the profit was nil (indicating that wealth was unchanged), even though the amount of cash decreased.

This highlights a very important issue in business. For a regular business to survive, it needs two things – it needs to make a profit to provide a return to its investors, but it also needs to generate cash flow to pay its expenses as they arise.

Even if you are generating a loss, you can continue to trade if you have adequate cash flow. However, if you run out of cash, the game is over! It's a simple rule – no cash, no business.

 The bare bones
There are two essential criteria for a regular trading business to survive:
* **It must generate profit**
* **It must generate cash flow**

Stripping it down to basics...

Sound financial management is a prerequisite for business success. The role of financial management in most businesses is to translate business ideas into profit. Profit should not be confused with cash flow:

* **Profit measures changes in wealth**
* **Cash flow measures changes in cash balances**

Given that these two concepts are not measuring the same thing, the way they are calculated differs:

* Profit is calculated by identifying the sales in a period and deducting the costs incurred to produce that period's sales.
* Cash flow is calculated by identifying the cash received in a period and deducting the cash paid out in the same period.

A regular trading business must generate both profit and cash flow if it is to survive.

3 HOW DO YOU MAKE PROFIT?

You may frequently hear people in your company saying 'We must make more profit!' – but how can this be done? If you have a clearer understanding of how your business makes profit, you can take positive steps to enhance its future performance.

The easiest way to understand how any business makes a profit is to view it as a process. Taking this approach, actions that will enhance future profitability become evident. **In this chapter we are going to examine the profit-making process and how it can be broken down into a series of clearly identifiable stages.**

Where does the profit-making process start?

The reason most businesses exist is to provide a return to their investors. Consequently, the profit-making process starts with investors providing funds at the start of the year and finishes with the business declaring a profit at the end of the year. Although in this chapter we are going to talk about the process as it applies within a company, the process is identical within an unincorporated business. Simply substitute the word 'investors' whenever you see the word 'shareholders.'

To identify where management can have an impact, the process can be divided into a series of discrete steps. Understanding and managing each step form a prerequisite to achieving financial success. Regrettably, many businesses fail simply because they do not under-

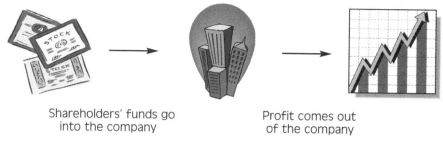

Shareholders' funds go
into the company

Profit comes out
of the company

PROVIDING A RETURN TO SHAREHOLDERS

stand the profit-making process. It is akin to trying to build a television system without knowing anything about electronics.

What we have established so far is that, in order to run a profitable company, shareholders' funds need to be raised at the outset.

Why do companies need shareholders?

Most people will tell you shareholders are essential because, without their funding, a company could not trade. This is not true. You can run a business without having to raise any funds from investors at all.

Suppose you have discovered a great new product: edible crockery. When people have finished their meal there's no need to wash up – they eat the plate with their coffee! Having canvassed friends and colleagues there seems to be a healthy market for this product, so you set up the Edible Plate Company. Being the shrewd businessperson you are, you insist on payment with each order and manage to secure orders totalling $60,000. You then contact a supplier and arrange for plates to be shipped directly to your customers. The supplier charges you $50,000 for this service, leaving you with a profit of $10,000. These transactions are summarized overleaf.

Insisting that customers pay cash with their orders means you do not need to raise any funds from investors. Your customers are financing the entire operation. This proves it is possible to start up a business without the need for investors. Regrettably, this is an extremely rare occurrence!

 **Customers** give you $60,000

out of which you pay $50,000 to the **supplier**

 who sends **plates** to your customers

leaving you $10,000 **profit**

EDIBLE PLATE COMPANY – CASH WITH ORDER

Let's revisit this business with a slight timing adjustment. Instead of requesting cash with the order, you are happy to be paid cash on delivery. This means you have to buy the plates from the supplier at the outset at a cost of $50,000. You then sell these plates to your customers for $60,000, leaving, as previously, a profit of $10,000 (see opposite).

In this latter scenario you need to raise $50,000 in order to commence trading. You may provide these funds yourself or raise at least some of the funds from other investors. This is in stark contrast to the original scenario where no initial investment was required. The reason you now need these funds is to purchase plates. Plates are an asset, where the term 'asset' simply means something you own.

So companies need shareholders to finance assets. The more assets a company needs, the more funds have to be raised. This can make or break a business. Suppose when setting up the Edible Plate Company you decide you want luxurious offices, an expensive car, cutting-edge computer equipment, and top-quality office furniture. In other words, you want lots of assets. This means you will need to raise a lot of funds to finance these assets. Lots of funding demands a high level of profit to provide a decent rate of return on that fund-

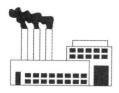

You pay $50,000 to the **supplier**

who gives you **plates**

 which you sell to **customers** for $60,000

leaving you $10,000 **profit**

EDIBLE PLATE COMPANY – CASH ON DELIVERY

ing. To achieve a high level of profit requires lots of sales. You have just managed to put enormous pressure on your sales figure and you have not even started trading yet. By contrast, if you start up your business with minimal assets, you will require minimal funding, which means only low levels of profit needed to provide a decent rate of return to the investors. This, in turn, means you will only need a low level of sales.

A common problem is that many people believe running a profitable business is all about sales and costs and therefore do not appreciate the significance of funding assets. This raises a question: If shareholders finance assets, how are all the other expenses paid for? Expenses such as salaries, telephone, stationery, and rent are all paid for out of sales. Sales do not only enable a business to make profit, they also provide the funds required to pay normal day-to-day expenses. This reinforces the point that shareholders only finance assets.

Shareholders
finance
assets

Sales
finance
expenses

FINANCING A BUSINESS

Why do companies borrow?

There is another way to finance assets – borrow the money. Why would any company want to borrow money if it can raise it from shareholders? If a business raises money from shareholders and fails to make a profit, there is no obligation to pay dividends. If it borrows money, it has to pay interest regardless of whether a profit is made or not. This would seem to suggest that companies should always raise funds from shareholders and resist the temptation to borrow. However, there is a very strong commercial argument for borrowing money and it is one that is not at all obvious. By borrowing money companies can increase the rate of return to shareholders. This is a very subtle tool that many businesses utilize to improve their profitability, but it does need explanation.

Let us return to the Edible Plate Company, where you invested $50,000 in order to buy plates, which you subsequently sold for $60,000, leaving a $10,000 profit. Delivering a $10,000 profit on a $50,000 investment represents a 20% rate of return. In other words, on every $100 invested, a profit of $20 is made. Of course, investors would welcome any opportunity to improve this rate of return. Borrowing additional funds provides such an opportunity. Suppose, in addition to raising $50,000 from shareholders, you decide to borrow $50,000 from a bank. You now have $100,000 to spend on plates. Given that you were previously able to sell $50,000 worth of plates for $60,000, you should be able to sell these plates for $120,000. However, the downside to having borrowed $50,000 is that you have to pay interest. If you are being charged 10% on the loan, this means the interest payable will be $5,000. So out of a sales figure of $120,000, you pay $100,000 for plates and $5,000 in interest, leaving $15,000 profit.

You raise
$50,000 from **shareholders** + $50,000 from a bank as a **loan**

which you pay to the **supplier**

who gives you **plates**

which you sell to **customers** for $120,000

out of which you pay $5,000 **interest**

leaving you $15,000 **profit**

EDIBLE PLATE COMPANY – PARTLY FINANCED BY A LOAN

Comparing this scenario against the previous one, profit has increased from $10,000 to $15,000, while funds raised from shareholders remain unchanged at $50,000. This represents a 30% rate of return. In the previous scenario, where $50,000 was raised from shareholders but no borrowing took place, the rate of return achieved was 20%.

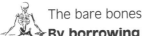

The bare bones

By borrowing money, companies can increase the rate of return provided on shareholders' funds.

Many companies are enticed by this argument and have borrowed money on the premise that it will result in improved returns to shareholders. However, there are two significant risks attached to borrowing money.

In the most recent example of your edible crockery business where you took out a $50,000 loan, the interest rate was assumed to be 10%. If the rate of interest increased to 20%, the interest payable would be $10,000. Should this occur, out of a sales figure of $120,000, you would still be spending $100,000 on plates but, after paying $10,000 interest, profit would be $10,000. Given shareholders' funds of $50,000, this would result in the rate of return falling back down to 20%. This is the same rate you were earning on sales of $60,000 with no borrowings at all. It follows that if the rate of interest increased beyond 20%, the rate of return would be less than if the company had not borrowed funds in the first place. Some companies overcome this problem by borrowing money at a fixed rate of interest. In other words, the interest rate is agreed for the duration of the loan. This does not overcome the second risk associated with borrowing money.

The more a business borrows, the more sensitive it is to changes in sales. In your edible crockery business, when you raise $50,000 from shareholders and borrow $50,000 at an interest rate of 10%, the rate of return is 30%. This assumes that sales of $120,000 are achieved. Suppose you sell all your inventory for $115,000. You will still be paying $100,000 for the plates and $5,000 in interest, leaving a profit of $10,000. Given that shareholders invested $50,000, this would result in a rate of return of 20%, which is the same as you would have achieved on sales of $60,000 with no borrowed funds at all. If you sold all your plates for $114,000 (you are just $6,000 below your target of $120,000), the rate of return would now be lower than it would have been if no loan had been taken out in the first place. So missing the sales plan by just $6,000 would result in the shareholders being worse off. This is the most potent risk that has to be confronted when bor-

rowing money. Raising funds in the form of borrowing is only beneficial if management has a high degree of confidence in its sales forecasts. Failure to achieve adequate sales could result in a dramatic
downturn in the rate of return being achieved.

 The bare bones

**Increasing borrowing within a company has two
potential risks:**
*   **The cost of borrowing could increase**
*   **The business is vulnerable to any downturn in
    sales**

We have now identified the first stage in the profit-making
process. Funds are raised to finance assets, where these can be raised
from shareholders and also in the form of borrowings. The more assets
a business needs, the more funding it requires. So when setting up a
company, you need to address two questions at the outset:

*   **What assets does the business need in order to trade?**
*   **How are these assets to be financed?**

The answers to these two questions will have a direct impact on
the rate of return the business achieves.

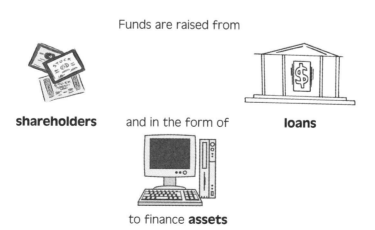

Funds are raised from

shareholders   and in the form of   **loans**

to finance **assets**

THE FIRST STAGE OF THE PROFIT-MAKING PROCESS:
RAISING FUNDS TO FINANCE ASSETS

Why do companies need assets?

Having established that funds are needed to finance assets, we now need to determine why companies need assets in the first place. The function of assets is to generate sales. Whether money is being invested in inventory, equipment, vehicles, buildings, or computer systems, the objective is to help the company generate sales. If assets underperform in this respect, this will adversely affect the rate of return being achieved for shareholders, which ultimately could lead to the company's demise.

Let's revisit the Edible Plate Company, where you raised $50,000 from shareholders plus a further $50,000 in the form of a bank loan. The various transactions entered into are reproduced opposite.

In total you raise $100,000 to finance assets (plates), which you subsequently sell for $120,000. The more sales you can generate from any given level of assets, the more effectively the assets are being utilized. We have now identified the second stage in the profit-making process: turning assets into sales.

Assets are required

to produce **sales**

**THE SECOND STAGE OF THE PROFIT-MAKING PROCESS:
TURNING ASSETS INTO SALES**

You raise
$50,000 from **shareholders** + $50,000 from a bank as a **loan**

which you pay to the **supplier**

who gives you **plates**

which you sell to **customers** for $120,000

out of which you pay $5,000 **interest**

leaving you $15,000 **profit**

EDIBLE PLATE COMPANY – REVISITED

Why are companies obsessed with sales?

The reason companies want sales is to generate profit. If sales this year are 50% up on last year, this may sound impressive. However, if profit is unaltered, the business is working harder but to no effect.

Let's take another look at your edible crockery business. You made a profit of $15,000 from sales of $120,000. Obviously, the more profit made from any given level of sales, the better the business is doing. This is the third (and final) stage in the profit-making process: turning sales into profit.

Sales are required

to produce **profit**

THE THIRD STAGE OF THE PROFIT-MAKING PROCESS:
TURNING SALES INTO PROFIT

Effective financial management involves managing all three stages of the profit-making process. Focusing attention on just one or two stages is no guarantee of success.

Stripping it down to basics...

Shareholders finance assets in the hope of achieving a return on their investment. How companies achieve this can be viewed as a three-stage process (as shown opposite):

* STAGE 1 **Raising funds to finance assets**
* STAGE 2 **Turning assets into sales**
* STAGE 3 **Turning sales into profit**

Funds can be raised from shareholders or by borrowing. An advantage of borrowing money is that it can increase the rate of return to shareholders. However, this strategy has two potential risks associated with it:

* **The cost of borrowing could increase**
* **The business is vulnerable to any downturn in sales**

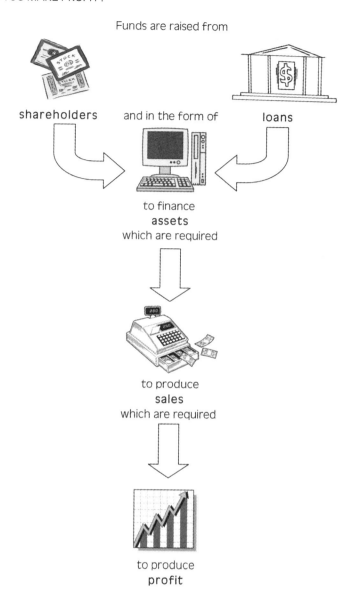

Funds are raised from

shareholders   and in the form of   loans

to finance
assets
which are required

to produce
sales
which are required

to produce
profit

THE PROFIT-MAKING PROCESS

Regardless of how the funds are raised, delivering a healthy rate of return on investors' funds demands the effective management of all three stages of the profit-making process.

4 HOW DO YOU
MEASURE FINANCIAL SUCCESS?

Your company's half-year results have just been announced. Sales have increased by 20% compared with the same period in the previous year, while profit has increased by 30%. Indeed, the reported profit of $6 million is the highest ever recorded in any six-month trading period. The employees are elated and yet it appears that the directors are despondent. They are not at all impressed with the figures – there is no pleasing some people!

Although sales and profit are central to success in any business, they are not objectives in themselves: they are means to an end. To manage the finances of a business you need to understand the measures used to assess performance. **In this chapter we are going to look at how to evaluate the financial performance of a business, both from an investor's point of view and a manager's point of view.**

How do shareholders measure success?

Profit is required to provide a return to the investors in the business. Does this mean that the objective is to make as much profit as possible? Let's start by looking at the problem from a shareholder's point of view.

When you buy shares in a company, you receive a share certificate that entitles you to a share of future profits. There are two ways you can benefit if you do this. First, you can receive a dividend, which is a payment of profit into your bank account. Second, the value of your shares can increase as the business becomes more successful. The total return you achieve during a year is a combination of these two factors.

Suppose you buy $1,000 worth of shares. During the following year you receive dividends totalling $50 and the value of the shares increases by $150. Your overall return on your $1,000 investment is $200 (comprising the $50 dividend plus the $150 increase in the value of the shares).

Shareholders
invest funds in

companies
that provide two potential benefits

dividends   **increasing
share values**

THE BENEFITS OF BEING A SHAREHOLDER

 The bare bones

Shareholders can benefit two ways by investing in a company:

   ✳   **Receiving a dividend**
   ✳   **The value of the shares increasing**

As a shareholder, you naturally want to keep up to date with how the company is doing. The problem is whenever companies report their results, they tend to focus on two issues: sales and profit. Do these provide a reasonable measure of their performance? For example, which of the following businesses would you suggest is more successful?

M T Drains
Maintenance Company

Sales $6,000,000
Profit $1,000,000

International
Piping Corporation

Sales $570,000,000
Profit Nil

WHICH IS MORE IMPORTANT – SALES OR PROFIT?

The maintenance company with sales of $6 million makes a profit – and therefore a return to its investors – of $1 million. By contrast, the piping corporation with sales of $570 million fails to provide any return to investors at all. Based on current performance, from an investor's point of view, the maintenance company is clearly the more attractive investment.

This highlights a very important point: sales do not provide a reasonable measure of financial success. When a company has high sales but no profit, its managers and staff may be working hard but to no effect. This has led to a frequently quoted expression:

Sales is vanity, profit is sanity!

Does this mean that profit is a more effective measure of success than sales? Let's examine a couple of typical headlines.

Grofast sees profits increase by 30% in a year!

Maykmore reports highest profits in its history!

WHICH IS MORE IMPORTANT: PROFIT GROWTH OR THE LEVEL OF PROFIT?

The Grofast headline comments on profit growth, while the Maykmore headline comments on the level of profit achieved. Which is more important?

To answer this, you need to think like an investor. Let's keep it simple. You open a savings account with a bank. If the bank pays you $200 interest at the end of the year, would you say that was good or bad performance? Based on the information provided so far, it is impossible to say – you need to know how much you have invested.

Suppose you have invested $1,000 during the year. Given this information, you may conclude that $200 interest represents a good rate of return. However, if you have invested $1 million, $200 interest may be regarded as a very poor rate of return. In both scenarios the amount of interest is unchanged (it is still $200), but your perception of performance differs markedly. This is because what you are interested in is the rate of return being achieved, not the absolute level of interest. The principle is identical when looking at a company.

A profit figure on its own does not tell us very much, no matter how it is expressed. Being told that profit is growing quickly or is at record levels tells us nothing about the rate of return being achieved. So where can you find out about a company's rate of return? Banks regularly advertise rates of return available on their savings accounts, but you won't find an advertisement for a company saying, 'Invest in Megabucks Inc. and earn 20% a year!'

Companies produce an annual report that provides details of their operations during the preceding year. This tells shareholders what the company has done with their money. It is common practice, particularly for companies that are quoted on a public stock exchange, to include a page providing financial highlights. This is the directors' opportunity to show off: they want to tell you about all their achievements. As a result, the principle appears to be: 'Why only show one figure, when you can show a whole page full!' A typical financial highlights page is shown overleaf.

This shows remarkable restraint – it only contains six figures. If ever you are tempted to look at the financial highlights in a real annual report, don't be surprised if you see 50 or more figures. The problem is to identify the figure that really counts. Let's work through the numbers shown here.

Nuway Trading Inc.
Financial Highlights for the Year Ended...

Sales	$275,600,000
Gross profit	$155,800,000
Operating profit	$45,200,000
Profit after tax	$29,500,000
Dividends per share	$1.28
Earnings per share	$3.75

* We have already discounted sales as an effective measure of business performance.
* We also noted that the absolute level of profit, no matter how it is defined (three variations are shown here), is not much use on its own.
* Moving on to dividends, these represent cash payments into a shareholder's bank account. Surely this is important? It may surprise you to hear that some companies don't pay dividends as a matter of policy. Despite this, shareholders are still keen to purchase their shares. If a company is displaying strong share price growth, even if it is not paying dividends, it can still prove to be an attractive investment. As a result, although dividends are often regarded as important, they are not the single most important issue.
* This leaves us with one figure: 'earnings per share' (commonly abbreviated to EPS). From a shareholder's perspective, this is the most critical measure of company performance.

 The bare bones
Shareholders measure profit performance in terms of earnings per share (EPS).

Don't underestimate what we have just said. Shareholders are not motivated by absolute levels of profit, they are motivated by earnings per share. To understand why this is so important, we need to look at how it is calculated. Earnings per share looks at the profit earned by a company and divides it by the number of shares issued to shareholders:

$$\text{Earnings per share} = \frac{\text{Profit}}{\text{Number of shares issued}}$$

Profit in this calculation refers to the profit available to shareholders. In other words, it is the profit made after paying for all the costs of running the business.

Suppose you have shares in a company that has made $10 million profit during the last year and has issued 2 million shares. The earnings per share is as follows:

$$\text{Earnings per share} = \frac{\$10 \text{ million profit}}{2 \text{ million shares}} = \$5.00$$

On every share you hold, the company has made you a profit of $5.00. From your perspective, this is far more useful than knowing that the company has made $10 million profit in total. However, this does not mean you are necessarily going to see $5.00 per share arriving in your bank account. It is the same as earning interest on a savings account. When you earn interest you have a choice: you can withdraw the interest now or leave it in the account so you can earn more interest next year. As a shareholder, you have the same two options: withdraw the profit now (as a dividend) or reinvest it back in the company in the hope of making more profit in the future. Earnings per share is the combined value of these two options.

Earnings per share   Dividend per share   Reinvested profit per share

EARNINGS PER SHARE COMPRISES TWO ELEMENTS

Ideally, investors want to see earnings per share increasing each year, but increasing earnings per share is not the same thing as increasing profit. Suppose you have shares in Hoe-Pless Industries. Two years ago it had 1 million shares in issue and made $3 million profit, providing earnings per share of $3. At the start of last year, the company issued another 1 million shares in order to raise additional finance and annual profit increased to $4 million. Is this good news for you as a shareholder? Although the company has made $4 million profit, it now has to spread this over 2 million shares, thereby reducing earnings per share to $2. So although profit has increased, your earnings per share has fallen from $3 to $2. This suggests that you were better off when the company made $3 million profit than when it made $4 million profit.

In practice, earnings per share in the short term can be volatile and situations such as that just described are not uncommon. Consequently, most shareholders tend to focus their attention on long-term growth in earnings per share. Providing this is being achieved, short-term fluctuations will not be viewed unfavorably.

So in order to keep shareholders happy, companies need to concentrate on increasing earnings per share, which is not necessarily the same as increasing profit. In fact, if you want to write a job description for a director of a company, you can do it in one line: 'Increase earnings per share.'

> **COMPANY DIRECTOR**
> Job Description
>
> Increase earnings per share!

How do managers measure success?

How can companies enhance earnings per share? Let's revisit how EPS is calculated:

$$\text{Earnings per share} = \frac{\text{Profit}}{\text{Number of shares issued}}$$

This ratio comprises two elements: the amount of profit made and the number of shares in issue. When a company sets a profit target for the year this will directly affect the way the business is managed. If it is an aggressive target, management will be under pressure to generate lots of sales and keep a firm grip on costs. If it is an easy target managers can be more relaxed because, even if sales fall slightly or costs start to increase, the profit target will still be achieved.

Now let's turn our attention to the other determinant of earnings per share: the number of shares in issue. What effect does this have on how a company is run? The answer is simple – it doesn't! Most managers probably haven't got a clue how many shares are in issue in their company; nor do they care. Earnings per share is an investors' measure: shareholders want to know how much profit is being earned on each share they hold. This is of no relevance to managers (unless, of course, they are also shareholders).

From a managerial viewpoint, what is relevant is the funds received in exchange for the shares. When shareholders invest $5 million in a company, for example, its managers must decide what they are going to do with that $5 million. This does affect how the business is managed. It follows that managers find it far more useful to look at profit in relation to shareholders' funds invested, rather than in relation to the number of shares in issue. This has led to the development of a measure known as 'return on equity' (often abbreviated to ROE), which looks at profit as a percentage of shareholders' funds:

$$\text{Return on equity} = \frac{\text{Profit}}{\text{Shareholders' funds}} \times 100\%$$

A SMALL MATHEMATICAL POINT
Whenever a calculation ends with the expression 'x 100%', this means that the result should be multiplied by 100. In other words, it should be expressed as a percentage (literally 'per one hundred').

'Return' is just another word for profit, while 'equity' is an alternative term for the owners' money invested in the business.

If a company makes $1 million profit during a year and the value of shareholders' funds is $5 million, return on equity can be calculated as follows:

$$\text{Return on equity} = \frac{\$1,000,000 \text{ profit}}{\$5,000,000 \text{ shareholders' funds}} \times 100\% = 20\%$$

On every $100 invested, the company has generated $20 profit during the year.

Return on equity is the most useful measure of profit performance available to managers. It certainly has far more intuitive appeal than earnings per share. Suppose a company is currently attaining an earnings per share of $0.80. To decide if this is good or bad performance, you need to compare it against previous years' figures. By contrast, a return on equity of 20% can be readily compared against rates of return being provided on alternative forms of investment. If regular savings accounts offer 5% interest per annum, a return on equity of 20% might be deemed a reasonable rate of return to compensate for the risk inherent in shares. Of course, a return on equity of 3% in this circumstance would not be viewed so favorably.

In essence, return on equity and earnings per share are just different ways of looking at the same problem. As a shareholder you talk about earnings per share (EPS), but as a manager you talk about return on equity (ROE). The logic is that if management focuses attention on providing a healthy return on equity, this should result in a healthy earnings per share for shareholders.

The bare bones
Managers measure profit performance in terms of return on equity (ROE).

Shareholders talk about
earnings per share

Managers talk about
return on equity

MEASURING PROFIT PERFORMANCE IN COMPANIES

A huge advantage of return on equity is that it can be applied within any type of business. It doesn't matter whether the business is being run as a sole trader, a partnership or a company, the objective is always the same – to provide a decent rate of return on the funds invested. The only difference when calculating return on equity for an unincorporated business is that the term 'shareholders' funds' must be replaced by the term 'investors' funds', where the latter refers to the total funds that the owners have invested in the business:

$$\text{Return on equity} = \frac{\text{Profit}}{\text{Investors' funds}} \times 100\%$$

If you invest $400,000 of your own money in a business that subsequently makes a profit during the next year of $60,000, your return on equity can be readily calculated:

$$\text{Return on equity} = \frac{\$60,000 \text{ profit}}{\$400,000 \text{ investors' funds}} \times 100\% = 15\%$$

On every $100 you have invested, a profit of $15 has been generated during the year.

Are there other commonly used measures of success?

As we have seen, every business has the opportunity to raise funds from two different sources:

* **Investors**
* **Borrowing**

This has led to the development of a variety of profitability measures in addition to earnings per share and return on equity.

Probably the most common alternative measure encountered in practice is 'return on capital employed' (often abbreviated to ROCE).

This is very different from return on equity and the argument for its existence runs as follows. Regardless of whether money is raised from shareholders or borrowed, management should be endeavoring to achieve the highest possible rate of return on all funds raised. To assess how effectively this is being done, return on capital employed looks at the return (profit) achieved in relation to the total capital employed in the business, where 'capital employed' is just another term for total funds raised:

$$\text{Return on capital employed} = \frac{\text{Profit}}{\text{Total funds raised}} \times 100\%$$

To understand the difference between return on equity and return on capital employed, let's revisit the operating results for Nuway Trading.

Nuway Trading Inc.
Financial Highlights for the Year Ended...

Sales	$275,600,000
Gross profit	$155,800,000
Operating profit	$45,200,000
Profit after tax	$29,500,000
Dividends per share	$1.28
Earnings per share	$3.75

Regardless of whether we are calculating return on equity or return on capital employed, we need two figures: a profit figure and a funds invested figure. Although we will be studying a variety of profit definitions in a later chapter, let's introduce two now:

* **Operating profit**
  Operating profit refers to the profit the company has made after paying all its running costs, but before it has paid interest on borrowed funds and before it has declared a profit available for shareholders.

✳ **Profit after tax**
Profit after tax refers to the profit that has been made exclusively for shareholders.

Now let's turn our attention to how Nuway Trading has funded its operations. Suppose this has been achieved as follows:

Shareholders' funds	$295,000,000
Borrowed funds	$270,000,000
TOTAL FUNDS RAISED	$565,000,000

There are two ways we can look at the return achieved on the funds raised. First there is return on equity, where we look at the profit available to shareholders (profit after tax) of $29.5 million in relation to the shareholders' funds of $295 million:

$$\text{ROE} = \frac{\text{Profit of } \$29,500,000}{\text{Shareholders' funds of } \$295,000,000} \text{ x } 100\% = 10\%$$

For every $100 of funds provided by shareholders, a profit of $10 is generated.

Return on capital employed focuses on the profit being made on all funds raised, regardless of whether they have been raised from shareholders or borrowed. In this instance, it is appropriate to look at the profit being made for all providers of finance. In other words, we want to look at the profit being made before paying interest on borrowed funds and before declaring a profit for shareholders. This needs to be examined in relation to the total funds raised. Using these figures, Nuway Trading generated an operating profit of $45.2 million on total funds of $565 million:

$$\text{ROCE} = \frac{\text{Profit of } \$45,200,000}{\text{Total funds raised of } \$565,000,000} \text{ x } 100\% = 8\%$$

On every $100 raised (regardless of whether it has been raised from investors or borrowed), the company produces a profit of $8, which will be used to provide a return to the lenders of finance (in the form of interest) and to shareholders (which they can either withdraw as a dividend or reinvest back in the business).

Which is more important: the fact the company is earning a 10% return on shareholders' funds or an 8% return on the total funds raised? Ultimately, return on equity is the more important measure, since it is the shareholders who own the business. However, return on capital employed does provide a useful measure of managerial efficiency. Given that your average manager is not informed whether the funds available have been raised from shareholders or borrowed, there is logic in the argument that managers should be seen to be maximizing the rate of return on all funds utilized. Don't let this divert you, however, from the primary financial objective, to provide a healthy return to shareholders; that is, to produce a healthy return on equity.

The bare bones

Return on capital employed (ROCE) measures how effective managers are at utilizing funds to generate profit, regardless of how these funds have been raised.

Stripping it down to basics...

Shareholders can benefit two ways by investing in a company:

* **Receiving a dividend**
* **The value of their shares increasing**

These benefits rely on the company's ability to deliver profit. Two measures are commonly used to assess how effective a company is at achieving this:

* **Shareholders measure profit performance in terms of earnings per share (EPS)**

✳ **Managers measure profit performance in terms of return on equity (ROE)**

Both measures assess returns to shareholders. The advantage of return on equity is that it can also be applied within unincorporated businesses.

Another measure that may be encountered is return on capital employed (ROCE), which assesses how effective managers are at utilizing funds to generate profit, regardless of whether these funds have been raised from shareholders or borrowed.

5 WHICH ARE THE FIGURES THAT COUNT?

Trying to keep track of the various issues being discussed in your company and fighting your way through all the reports that are produced on a daily basis can at times appear to be an insurmountable task. What you want to know is, out of all the figures produced, which are the ones that count?

The good news is that most businesses can be reduced to the management of just four numbers, thereby making financial management far more straightforward and more focused. **In this chapter we are going to identify what the four key figures are in a business and what actions management can take to improve them.**

What are the four key figures in a business?

In Chapter 2 ('Is it all about profit?'), we identified two essential criteria for a business to succeed commercially:

* **It must generate profit**
* **It must generate cash flow**

In Chapter 3 ('How do you make profit?'), we noted that there are three stages to managing a profitable business:

✳ **Raising funds to finance assets**
✳ **Turning assets into sales**
✳ **Turning sales into profit**

In Chapter 4 ('How do you measure financial success?'), we were introduced to return on equity as a measure that can be applied within any business to assess how effectively investors' funds are being turned into profit.

Let's consolidate these concepts. The first stage of the profit-making process is all about raising cash from shareholders and in the form of borrowings in order to finance assets. The second stage is all about turning these assets back into cash in the form of sales. These first two stages are therefore all about cash management. It is only the third stage that is true profit management: ensuring that the sales generated result in increased wealth for the shareholders. Return on equity provides a measure that allows us to assess how effectively the entire process is being managed. This places us in a position to develop a coherent view of any business.

STAGE IN PROFIT-MAKING PROCESS	IMPACT ON CASH AND PROFIT	PERFORMANCE MEASURE
Raising funds to finance assets	} Cash management	} Return on equity
Turning assets into sales		
Turning sales into profit	} Profit management	

A common failing in many businesses is an obsession with profit management while disregarding cash management. Given that two out of the three stages in the profit-making process hinge on cash management, this explains why many companies run into cash-flow difficulties. It is impossible to generate a sustainable return on equity without sound management of both cash flow and profit. This is because return on equity links the two concepts: it looks at how effectively cash raised from investors is being turned into profit.

Having a coherent view of a business enables us to identify the four key figures that drive it. To do this, let's revisit the Edible Plate Company, introduced in Chapter 3, where you raised $50,000 from shareholders and $50,000 as a loan.

You raise

$50,000 from **shareholders** + $50,000 from a bank as a **loan**

which you pay to the **supplier**

who gives you **plates**

which you sell to **customers** for $120,000

out of which you pay $5,000 **interest**

leaving you $15,000 **profit**

EDIBLE PLATE COMPANY – REVISITED

Not surprisingly, the first issue we want to address is how effectively the business is being managed overall. This can be assessed in terms of return on equity:

$$\text{Return on equity} = \frac{\text{Profit of } \$15,000}{\text{Shareholders' funds of } \$50,000} \times 100\% = 30\%$$

When examining any business, this is the first key figure that ought to be looked at. Is the business providing an adequate return to shareholders? In this instance we are being told that, on every $100 raised from shareholders, a profit of $30 is being generated. This leads us on to the next logical question: How is this being achieved? Having established that there are three stages in the profit-making process, it will probably not surprise you to hear that there are three associated measures, one for each stage.

Let's start by looking at the first stage of the process: raising funds to finance assets. As we have seen, there are two ways a company can raise funds: from shareholders and in the form of borrowings. The relationship between these two sources of funds is known as 'gearing' (or 'leverage'). This tells us what proportion of funds raised to finance a business is in the form of borrowings. Although there are various ways gearing can be calculated, a common method is as follows:

$$\text{Gearing} = \frac{\text{Long-term borrowings}}{\text{Total long-term funds}} \times 100\%$$

To appreciate the significance of this calculation, you need to understand both components fully. The first point to note is that gearing is concerned with 'long-term borrowings.' This does not include short-term borrowings such as when a business agrees to pay its suppliers 30 days after goods are delivered. Gearing focuses on long-term borrowings on which interest is continually payable.

'Total long-term funds' refers to long-term borrowings plus long-term funds raised from shareholders. In your edible crockery business, you raise $50,000 from shareholders and borrow $50,000 from a bank. This provides total long-term funds of $100,000. We are now in a position to calculate gearing for the Edible Plate Company:

$$\text{Gearing} = \frac{\text{Long-term borrowings of } \$50,000}{\text{Total long-term funds of } \$100,000} \times 100\% = 50\%$$

Out of every $100 raised, $50 is borrowed. A business is referred to as 'high geared' if it has a gearing of more than 50% – the bulk of its funds is raised in the form of borrowings. A business is referred to as 'low geared' if it has a gearing of less than 50% – the bulk of its funds is raised from shareholders. If gearing is exactly 50% the company is referred to as 'gearing neutral'.

The bare bones
Gearing measures the proportion of long-term funds within a business that is borrowed.

The second stage of the profit-making process involves turning assets into sales. 'Asset turnover' assesses the ability of a business to generate turnover (which is just another word for sales) from the funds it has raised to finance its assets:

$$\text{Asset turnover} = \frac{\text{Sales}}{\text{Total long-term funds}}$$

In your edible crockery business, you raise $100,000 in total to invest in assets (plates), which you subsequently sell for $120,000:

$$\text{Asset turnover} = \frac{\text{Sales of } \$120,000}{\text{Total long-term funds of } \$100,000} = 1.2$$

From every $1 invested in assets, $1.20 worth of sales are generated. The higher the number, the more effectively assets are being utilized.

The bare bones
Asset turnover measures the ability of a business to turn assets into sales.

The third stage of the profit-making process is turning sales into profit. 'Profit margin' measures how effective a business is at achieving this:

$$\text{Profit margin} = \frac{\text{Profit}}{\text{Sales}} \times 100\%$$

In your edible crockery business, a profit is made of $15,000 from sales of $120,000:

$$\text{Profit margin} = \frac{\text{Profit of } \$15,000}{\text{Sales of } \$120,000} \times 100\% = 12.5\%$$

From every $100 of sales, a profit of $12.50 is made for shareholders. Obviously, the higher the percentage, the better the business is doing. However, what the profit margin is really commenting on is cost management. A profit margin of 12.5% tells us that out of every $100 sale, $87.50 is being spent running the business. If you want to increase the profit margin, you need to spend less than $87.50 to create a $100 sale.

The bare bones
Profit margin measures the ability of a business to turn sales into profit.

What we have now established is that return on equity in any business is a combination of gearing, asset turnover, and profit margin. These form the four key figures that can be used to assess any business. **Return on equity** tells us how the business is doing overall, while **gearing, asset turnover**, and **profit margin** tell us how this result is being achieved. However, these measures don't only tell us how the business is managing the profit-making process, they also comment on how profit and cash flow are being managed.

* **Return on equity**
  Measures how effectively **cash** raised from shareholders is being turned into **profit**.
* **Gearing**
  Measures how effectively **cash** is raised to finance assets.

✳ **Asset turnover**
Measures how effectively assets are used to generate **cash** in the form of sales.

✳ **Profit margin**
Measures how effectively sales are converted into **profit**.

Every business can be broken down into these four core elements.

How do the four key figures interrelate?

In your edible crockery business, a return on equity of 30% is delivered to the shareholders. We are now going to find out how this is achieved. Follow through the next few paragraphs slowly, as they bring together all the principles that underpin every type of business and, most importantly, show how they interrelate.

Stage 1 of the profit-making process: Raising funds to finance assets

Gearing in the Edible Plate Company is 50%, which tells us that out of every $100 raised to acquire assets, $50 is borrowed. Given that you raised $100,000 in total, it follows that half of this must have been borrowed:

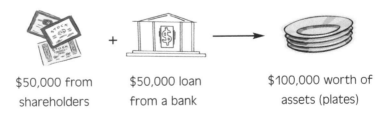

| $50,000 from | $50,000 loan | $100,000 worth of |
| shareholders | from a bank | assets (plates) |

Stage 2 of the profit-making process: Turning assets into sales

An asset turnover of 1.2 tells us that from every $1 invested in assets, $1.20 worth of sales are generated. Consequently, $100,000 invested in plates must have produced $120,000 worth of sales:

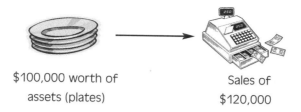

$100,000 worth of
assets (plates)

Sales of
$120,000

Stage 3 of the profit-making process: Turning sales into profit

A profit margin of 12.5% tells us that from every $100 of sales gener-
ated, $12.50 profit is made after paying for all costs. Given sales of
$120,000, it follows a profit of $15,000 must have been achieved
(being 12.5% of $120,000):

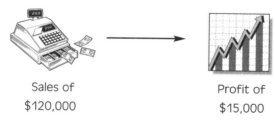

Sales of
$120,000

Profit of
$15,000

Following through these three stages it can be seen how shareholders' funds of $50,000 have produced a profit of $15,000, resulting
in a return on equity of 30%.

What strategies will enhance the profit-making process?

A benefit of having identified the four key figures in any business
is that it enables us to identify practical management action to
enhance performance.

Performance measure 1: Return on equity

The objective is to deliver a healthy return on equity and this is the
measure that should be constantly monitored to assess whether or not
any given strategy is working.

Performance measure 2: Gearing

Gearing examines the first stage of the profit-making process – the
amount and type of funds being raised to finance assets. There is only

one way it can be increased: increase the proportion of funds borrowed. This tends to be a periodic, one-off decision. Once the decision is made, it may be several months before the issue is looked at again. Indeed, this typically is addressed at board level and as a consequence does not tend to fall within the domain of day-to-day business management. It is very unlikely that your average manager goes into work thinking 'We must issue more shares' or 'We must borrow more funds.' What is far more relevant to managers is what to do with the funds once they have been raised.

It should be noted that although gearing is not a day-to-day management issue, it does affect day-to-day management. The advantage of gearing is that it enables return on equity potentially to be increased. However, this benefit is contingent on a company's ability to deliver adequate sales. The higher the gearing, the more critical the sales plan becomes and the more focused management must be on achieving this.

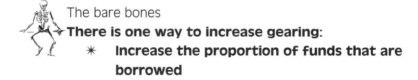

The bare bones

There is one way to increase gearing:
  * **Increase the proportion of funds that are borrowed**

Performance measure 3: Asset turnover

It is at this stage where management can have real impact: turning assets into sales. Don't underestimate the importance of asset turnover. A company might have $10 million worth of assets and a 90% profit margin, which might sound impressive to the uninitiated. However, if the company only generates $100 worth of sales during the year from all those assets, a 90% margin would mean it has made a grand total of $90 profit! Without a healthy asset turnover, profit margin is irrelevant.

Suppose you are invited to invest in a new company that is going to sell beachwear and it intends to open its first store in Northern Greenland. There are two problems here: there are no beaches in Northern Greenland; and there are unlikely to be any customers. In other words, the company is about to invest in the wrong assets:

* **It is going to invest in a store that is clearly in the wrong location**
* **It is going to invest in stock for which there is no demand**

No matter how tightly costs are controlled, the company is not going to provide a return to shareholders.

How can companies improve asset turnover? Let's remind ourselves how it is calculated:

$$\text{Asset turnover} = \frac{\text{Sales}}{\text{Total long-term funds}}$$

Given that long-term funds are used to finance assets, this suggests two ways asset turnover can be enhanced:

* **Increase sales from existing assets**
  This can be achieved by using assets more intensively. For example, the main asset in a department store business is the store itself. One way asset turnover could potentially be improved is by extending its trading hours, since more sales will be generated from the same asset.
* **Maintain current sales with fewer assets**
  This can be achieved by reducing the level of assets. For example, an important asset in many companies is accounts receivable. This refers to amounts owed by customers; you can own debts. If a company provides customers with 60 days' credit, the value of accounts receivable will be significant. By collecting amounts owed more promptly, the value of this asset will fall. Providing this can be achieved without losing sales, asset turnover will increase.

The bare bones
There are two ways to increase asset turnover:
  * **Increase sales from existing assets**
  * **Maintain current sales with less assets**

Performance measure 4: Profit margin

The ability to turn sales into profit is measured by the profit margin:

$$\text{Profit margin} = \frac{\text{Profit}}{\text{Sales}} \times 100\%$$

By spending less to achieve a $100 sale, profit per $100 sale will increase. This provides a strategy for increasing profit margin:

* **Reduce costs as a percentage of sales**

  You don't need to cut costs in order to improve this ratio. If sales are increasing, provided that costs don't grow as fast, costs as a percentage of sales will fall. For example, suppose payroll costs in a company are 20% higher than the previous year. If sales have increased by 30%, this will mean payroll costs as a percentage of sales will have fallen, thereby increasing the profit margin – well done! In fact, cutting costs might be the worst thing to do because, if this results in falling sales, the profit margin might fall.

This highlights an important difference between cost cutting and cost control:

* **Cost cutting means reducing costs**
* **Cost control means managing costs as a percentage of sales**

Any Neanderthal with a sloping head dragging his knuckles across the ground can cut costs for you, but who knows what the consequences will be! Cost control, by contrast, is something far more refined. It asks the question: 'Can we maintain sales and service levels, but at a lower cost base?'

A manager who cuts costs   A manager who controls costs

COST CUTTING VERSUS COST CONTROL

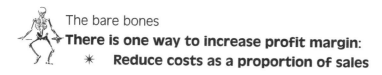

The bare bones
There is one way to increase profit margin:
* **Reduce costs as a proportion of sales**

By examining how the four key figures in a business interrelate, we have been able to identify three potential strategies for enhancing return on equity in the future. These can be summarized as follows:

* **Increase gearing**
  so that a greater proportion of funds is borrowed (although this will only succeed if adequate sales are achieved)
* **Improve asset turnover**
  so that more sales are generated from each $100 worth of assets
* **Improve profit margin**
  so that less is being spent to generate each $100 worth of sales

Stripping it down to basics...

There are four figures that count in any business:

* **Return on equity**
  measures how effectively cash raised from investors is turned into profit
* **Gearing**
  assesses how risky a business is, in terms of how it funds its assets
* **Asset turnover**
  measures the ability of a business to turn assets into sales
* **Profit margin**
  measures the ability of a business to turn sales into profit

Return on equity is the objective, while the other three measures provide the means of achieving this objective. Consequently, there are three strategies to enhance return on equity:

✳ **Increase gearing**
Increase the proportion of funds that are borrowed

✳ **Increase asset turnover**
Either Increase sales from existing assets
Or Maintain current sales with fewer assets

✳ **Increase profit margin**
Reduce costs as a percentage of sales

Part Two

USING FINANCIAL INFORMATION

To manage the finances of a business

you need to understand the information around you

6 WHY PRODUCE FINANCIAL STATEMENTS?

The rows of chrome and leather-effect chairs provide a stark contrast to the Picasso prints decorating the walls. Mobile phone ringtones are a constant companion as people take their seats. On your chair there is a set of papers neatly stapled in the top left-hand corner. The Aardvark Trading logo stands proudly on the front page, below which appear the words 'Annual Review of Results.' A cough from the front stage indicates that the chief executive is to commence his address. A flurry of activity ensues as telephones are switched to silent mode.

The presentation is inspiring. The chief executive enthuses about the products, congratulates the staff on their efforts, expounds a vision for the future, and even manages to squeeze in a couple of mildly amusing jokes. Then come the words that everyone dreads: 'And now let me pass you over to our chief finance officer.' Visuals are projected behind the stage containing tables of numbers, graphs, formulae, and even a couple of poorly lit photographs of a supplier invoice. Throughout the presentation reference is continually made to AVA. This you later discover is an internal measure that has been devised by the finance team and stands for 'Aardvark Value Added,' although you're unable to find anyone who knows what it means. You spend most of the presentation studying one of the Picasso prints, trying to work out where he found a woman with one breast, two mouths, and a nose growing out of the side of her head. At one stage, one of your colleagues lets out a loud snort just as his unconscious head is about to touch his knee. Several people turn around disapprovingly and then redirect their attention back to counting the hairs growing out of people's ears, fantasizing about dating the newest employee, and guessing who has the most expensive suit in the room.

Why does the very mention of a financial presentation instill boredom in an audience even before it starts? If marketing executives had designed financial statements, they would no doubt be filled with dazzling images and memorable slogans. If information technology specialists had designed these documents, they would probably contain flow charts showing logically how all the parts of the business fit together. However, we have to face facts. Financial statements are designed by accountants, which means we have to make do with lengthy tables of figures coupled with technical jargon that most people don't understand.

Believe it or not, financial statements are inherently exciting documents because they tell you how a business has been trading. A set of annual accounts is a summary of everything a business has done during the previous year. Investors should be clamoring for these reports to find out what is happening to their wealth. Managers should be equally enthusiastic to find out how successful they have been at managing the business. Financial statements can tell you what is going right and what is going wrong. Although they may at first sight appear rather bland, you will discover you can extract a lot of valuable information in a very short period. **In this chapter we are going to examine the most commonly encountered financial statements, what they tell us about a business, and what all the jargon means.**

What is the role of financial statements?

Financial statements enable investors to assess how effective a business is at providing them with a return on their investment. It follows that these documents ought to be answering the questions investors want addressed. Therefore, to appreciate financial statements, you need to think like an investor.

What motivates investors is their rate of return. Simply being told how much profit a business has made during a period is not much use on its own. To decide whether or not this figure is satisfactory, they also need to know how much was invested. Consequently, if you are an investor, there are two fundamental questions you would like answered:

* **How much is invested in the business?**
  You want to know the **value** of your investment.
* **What return is being earned on the investment?**
  You want to know how much **profit** you are making.

However, making profit is not enough to ensure that a business is going to survive – it also needs cash flow. It follows that there is a third fundamental question you need answered:

* **What is happening to cash?**
  You want to be sure that there is adequate **cash flow** to pay the expenses as they arise.

You will not be surprised to hear that there are three financial statements that provide the answers to these questions:

* **For the value of the business look at the balance sheet**
* **To identify the profit made consult the income statement (also known as the profit and loss account)**
* **To see what is happening to cash flow turn to the cash flow statement**

These documents need to be produced on a regular basis, not only to keep investors informed of how the business is trading, but also to assist management in identifying where action is required.

In addition to investors and managers, there are other groups who like to see financial statements, for a variety of reasons. For example, suppliers may want to assess the ability of a business to pay before agreeing to offer credit terms. Customers may want to confirm the financial standing of a business before entering into a long-term contract. The government wants to know how much profit is being made to assess the liability to tax.

There are three key financial statements in any business:

 ✳ Balance sheet
 ✳ Income statement
 ✳ Cash flow statement

Balance sheet
answers the question
of value

Income statement
answers the question
of profit

Cash flow statement
answers the question
of cash flow

THE THREE KEY FINANCIAL STATEMENTS

Considerable diversity can be encountered in how businesses lay out their financial statements, both in terms of the format used and the level of detail provided. However, the principles underpinning each document never change. If you understand the principles, you should be able to pick up the financial statements of any business and make sense of the information being presented.

What does a balance sheet tell you?

When you are looking at the financial results of a company, you should start with the balance sheet, which answers the question: 'How much is invested in the business?' This is a powerful document: it tells you how much the business is worth. In other words, it is a calculation of wealth. To assess the performance of any type of investment, it is essential you start off by establishing how much you have invested.

Suppose you wanted to find out what you personally are worth today. You would probably start off by asking: 'What do I own?' Things you own might include bank accounts, a car, a house, furniture, and so on. These are your assets. The first stage in finding out what you are worth is to add up the value of all your assets.

The second stage of the valuation process involves asking the question most people try to avoid: 'What do I owe?' The amount you owe is called a 'liability,' whereas the company or individual you owe the money to is called a 'creditor.' When an electricity bill arrives for $300, the liability is $300 and the creditor is the electricity company. Amounts you personally owe might include a mortgage, a car loan, credit card bills, and utility bills.

By deducting what you owe from what you own, you can identify what you are worth – your wealth. This is all a balance sheet does: it adds up everything you own and deducts everything you owe. An example of a balance sheet for an individual is provided below.

BALANCE SHEET
FOR IVOR LOTT
AS AT 31 DECEMBER

$

ASSETS
House, car, furniture, savings, etc.   1,500,000

LESS LIABILITIES
Mortgage, credit card bills, utility bills, etc.   –1,000,000

WEALTH   500,000

A BALANCE SHEET FOR AN INDIVIDUAL

The first point to note on a balance sheet is the date. When you value something, it is always at a point in time. In this instance, we are determining what Ivor Lott is worth on 31 December. On that day, we can see that Ivor owns $1.5 million worth of assets but has liabilities of $1 million. As a result, he is worth the difference: $500,000.

The balance sheet of a company is no different to that of an individual. A company will add up what it owns and deduct what it owes, in order to determine how much it is worth. A company balance sheet will contain more detail than the document shown above, but the principles are the same.

 The bare bones
A balance sheet is a statement of wealth expressed in terms of what a business owns and what it owes.

There are two formats for balance sheets commonly encountered in practice, as shown below and overleaf.

MAYKEM & SELLEM INC.
BALANCE SHEET
AS AT 31 DECEMBER

	$ million
Fixed assets	78
Current assets	69
TOTAL ASSETS	147
LESS Current liabilities	-41
Long-term liabilities	−22
NET ASSETS	84
Capital	30
Reserves	54
SHAREHOLDERS' FUNDS	84

BALANCE SHEET – FORMAT 1

Both formats are presenting exactly the same information, the only difference is how it is laid out. If you can make sense of one format, you will also be able to make sense of the other. For expositional purposes, we will concentrate our attention on Format 1. At first glance this statement may look ominous; it is certainly a lot more complicated than the balance sheet we examined for Ivor Lott. The good news is that it is not as bad as it looks! As when trying to understand

MAYKEM & SELLEM INC.
BALANCE SHEET
AS AT 31 DECEMBER

	$ million
Current assets	69
Fixed assets	78
TOTAL ASSETS	147
Current liabilities	41
Long-term liabilities	22
TOTAL LIABILITIES	63
SHAREHOLDERS' FUNDS	
Capital	30
Reserves	54
LIABILITIES & SHAREHOLDERS' FUNDS	147

BALANCE SHEET – FORMAT 2

anything that appears a bit technical, it can be a lot easier to comprehend if it is broken up into sections. Let's take another look at this balance sheet, but now highlighting the main components (as shown opposite).

A balance sheet for a company comprises just four sections. The first three sections are very similar to a personal balance sheet. They examine:

* **What the company owns (its assets)**
* **What the company owes (its liabilities)**
* **What the company is worth (its wealth)**

We add up what we own, deduct what we owe and, on that basis, determine what we are worth. However, a company balance sheet provides an additional piece of information:

* **The value of the shareholders' investment**

MAYKEM & SELLEM INC.
BALANCE SHEET
AS AT 31 DECEMBER

	$ million	
Fixed assets	78	
Current assets	69	
TOTAL ASSETS	147	This is what the company owns
LESS Current liabilities	-41	
Long-term liabilities	-22	This is what the company owes
NET ASSETS	84	This is what the company is worth
Capital	30	
Reserves	54	
SHAREHOLDERS' FUNDS	84	This is the value of the shareholders' investment

BALANCE SHEET – A SIMPLIFIED VIEW

Let's examine each of these sections in turn. Before we do this, a word of warning: you are about to encounter a significant amount of jargon. The world of finance is littered with technical terms, many of which emanate from financial statements. Consequently, this chapter is also a language course.

Just as you do when you're calculating your personal wealth, the first thing a company does is add up the value of everything it owns. It is worth noting that it is common practice within most businesses to divide what they own into two types:

* **Fixed assets**
* **Current assets**

Fixed assets are assets that have been acquired with the intention of keeping them in their current form for more than one year. In other words, they are fixed in nature; hence the name. If a business buys several computers for use in an office, they are fixed assets – they have been acquired with the intention of keeping them in their current form for more than one year. By contrast, a computer manufacturer would not treat the computers it builds as fixed assets, since it intends to convert them into cash (through sales) in the near future. Consequently, what is a fixed asset in one business may not be a fixed asset in another. Examples of what many businesses deem to be fixed assets include (provided that they are owned and not rented) office buildings, equipment, and vehicles.

Current assets, if you want a really basic definition, comprise all assets that are not fixed! A more proactive definition would be anything a business owns that it intends to keep in its current form for less than one year. The three most common types of current asset encountered in practice are as follows:

* **Inventory**
  Businesses hold stocks of raw materials and finished goods with the intention of converting them into cash through sales.
* **Accounts receivable**
  Customer accounts where payment is outstanding are known as 'accounts receivable,' while the people who owe the money are called 'debtors.' Usually, accounts receivable are created when a business sells goods or services to a customer and payment is not required immediately. In other words, these are accounts where the company is to receive money in the future. The intention is to convert these accounts into cash by collecting the sums due.

* **Cash**
Businesses do not acquire cash to admire it, they acquire cash to spend it. In other words, the intention is to convert cash into goods and services.

By adding up all its fixed assets and all its current assets, a business can identify everything it owns. In the case of Maykem & Sellem, the balance sheet tells us the business has $78 million worth of fixed assets (e.g. buildings, equipment, and furniture) and $69 million worth of current assets (e.g. inventory, accounts receivable, and cash), giving it total assets of $147 million.

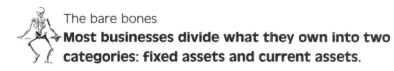

The bare bones
Most businesses divide what they own into two categories: fixed assets and current assets.

The next section of the balance sheet, just as if you were calculating your personal wealth, deducts what is owed. As with assets, liabilities within businesses are commonly divided into two types:

* **Current liabilities**
* **Long-term liabilities**

Current liabilities are amounts owed that are due for payment within 12 months from the balance sheet date. One group that businesses commonly owe a lot of money to are suppliers (e.g. suppliers of inventory or equipment) and the amounts owed to this group are commonly referred to as 'accounts payable.' These are accounts where the company has to pay out money in the future. Other types of current liability include short-term loans from banks and taxes payable to the government.

Long-term liabilities are amounts owed that are payable more than 12 months from the balance sheet date. They tend to comprise sources of long-term finance such as loans that extend over more than one year.

The balance sheet of Maykem & Sellem tells us that the company has $41 million worth of debts payable within the next year, plus a further $22 million worth of debts payable after one year.

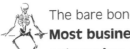 The bare bones
**Most businesses divide what they owe into two
categories: current liabilities and long-term liabilities.**

Having established what it owns and what it owes, the next section of the balance sheet tells us what the business is worth.

Net assets is another term for wealth and it is the difference
between what is owned and what is owed. The balance sheet of
Maykem & Sellem tells us the company has assets worth $147 million,
out of which it has to meet liabilities of $63 million, leaving the busi-
ness with net assets of $84 million.

The final section of the balance sheet examines the value of the
company from a shareholder's perspective. You will note that the value
of shareholders' funds is the same as the value of the net assets. This is
not a coincidence – it will always be the case. If Maykem & Sellem
closed down tomorrow, sold off all its assets, and paid off all its liabilities, the net assets figure in the balance sheet tells us that (in theory at
least) there would be $84 million left over. Who owns this money? The
answer is, the shareholders. In other words, if the net assets are valued
at $84 million, the shareholders must have $84 million invested in the
company. The final section of the balance sheet examines where the
$84 million of shareholders' funds has come from.

There are only two ways shareholders can finance a business:
they either invest cash in exchange for shares or they reinvest profit that
has been made.

As a result, the balance sheet divides shareholders' funds into
two elements:

* Capital
* Reserves

Capital represents the amount of money invested in a company
in exchange for shares. Given that a company may continue to issue
shares over many years, capital represents the total funds received by
the business in exchange for all shares that have been issued since it
started trading.

Reserves represent profit reinvested back into the company. The figure is the difference between the capital and the net assets. In the case of Maykem & Sellem, we have a company with capital of $30 million and net assets of $84 million. The value of reserves is the difference: $54 million. This tells us that, over the years, $30 million has been invested in exchange for shares. However, the business is now worth $84 million. In other words, the value (the wealth) of the company has increased by $54 million. For this to happen, it follows that the business must have made and subsequently reinvested profits of $54 million.

It is the same as you having a savings account into which you have invested $10,000 over the years. If the account now has a balance of $12,000, the difference between the current balance and the amount you invested over the years ($2,000) must be interest. This is not necessarily the total interest you have earned. Over the years you may have earned substantially more than $2,000 but decided to withdraw some of it from the account. The $2,000 difference only represents the interest you have reinvested.

Shareholders' funds represent the value of capital and reserves combined. An alternative title often encountered for these funds is 'stockholders' equity.'

The bare bones
Most businesses divide shareholders' funds into two categories: capital and reserves.

Let's summarize what we have learned from the balance sheet for Maykem & Sellem. Adding up everything the business owns and deducting everything the business owes tells us that the company has net assets worth $84 million. These have been financed by shareholders investing $30 million in exchange for shares and also reinvesting profit of $54 million.

Time for a piece of trivia! The fact that the net assets of a company and the shareholders' funds must by definition equate has led many people to believe that this is why the document is called a balance sheet. This is a misconception. The reason it is called a balance sheet is because it provides a list of balances (i.e. values). It asks: 'What

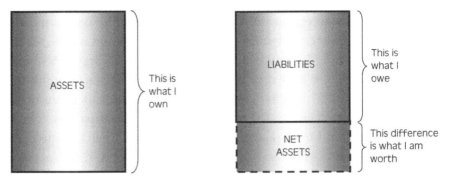

THE BALANCE SHEET IS A STATEMENT OF WEALTH

is the balance on our fixed assets?', 'What is the balance on our current assets?', and so on. Mystery solved!

What does an income statement tell you?

 To determine whether or not a profit is being made, we need to look to the income statement (or profit and loss account). This tells shareholders whether their wealth, as stated in the balance sheet, is moving up or down. To provide this information, we noted in Chapter 2 that profit has to be calculated in a very specific way:

Profit in a period = Sales in a period
                       LESS Costs incurred to produce that period's
                       sales

Profit adds up sales (regardless of when the cash is received) and deducts all the costs incurred to produce that period's sales (regardless of when cash is paid out).

When a profit is declared, the shareholders are being told that the value of their investment in the business has increased. Conversely, when a loss is declared, the shareholders are being told that the value of their investment has decreased.

The bare bones
An income statement states whether the wealth of a business is going up or down.

A typical company income statement might be presented as shown below.

MAYKEM & SELLEM INC.
INCOME STATEMENT
FOR THE YEAR ENDED 31 DECEMBER

		$ million
SALES		200
LESS	Cost of sales	−126
GROSS PROFIT		74
LESS	Operating costs	−54
OPERATING PROFIT		20
LESS	Interest payable	−2
PROFIT BEFORE TAX		18
LESS	Tax	−6
PROFIT AFTER TAX		12
LESS	Dividends	−4
RETAINED PROFIT		8

INCOME STATEMENT – THE INITIAL VIEW

As in the case of the balance sheet, this document can be simplified by breaking it down into sections (as shown overleaf).

The income statement can be seen as comprising four distinct sections:

MAYKEM & SELLEM INC.
INCOME STATEMENT
FOR THE YEAR ENDED 31 DECEMBER

$ million

Sales	200

These are the sales
achieved

LESS Cost of sales	-126
GROSS PROFIT	74
LESS Operating costs	-54

These are the
costs incurred

OPERATING PROFIT	20

This is the profit
achieved

LESS Interest payable	-2
PROFIT BEFORE TAX	18
LESS Tax	-6
PROFIT AFTER TAX	12
LESS Dividends	-4
RETAINED PROFIT	8

This is what the business
does with the profit

INCOME STATEMENT – A SIMPLIFIED VIEW

* **Sales**
* **Costs**
* **Profit**
* **What the business does with the profit**

Unlike the balance sheet, which provides a snapshot of the business at a point in time, the income statement summarizes what happens over a period of time. In the case of Maykem & Sellem it covers activity for the 12 months ended 31 December.

Let's explore each section of this statement in turn. As with the balance sheet, a certain amount of jargon is going to be encountered. This will help in making you fluent in the language of finance, so it's worth the effort.

Sales is the first figure encountered in an income statement. Alternative titles include 'turnover' and 'revenue.' During the year Maykem & Sellem generated sales of $200 million.

This raises an important issue. When should a sale be reported in the income statement: when the sale takes place or when the cash is received? The answer is when the sale takes place. The reason for this is that profit measures changes in wealth. When a company quotes a sales figure, it is claiming that its wealth has gone up. If a customer pays cash on delivery, the wealth of the company is seen to be going up because it is acquiring cash (which is an asset). However, if a sale is on credit, the company provides the customer with goods or services but payment is due at a later date. In this instance, the business still acquires an asset at the point of sale, an account receivable. The business has acquired a debt (which it owns), so the wealth of the business has still gone up. Consequently, the figure quoted represents the total value of sales achieved, regardless of whether the cash has been received or not.

The bare bones
Sales in an income statement comprise all sales arising during the period, regardless of whether cash has been received or not.

The next section of the income statement deducts the costs incurred to produce the sales during the period. Typically the costs of running a business are divided into two categories:

* Cost of sales
* Operating costs

In addition, between these two cost categories, a profit definition is introduced:

* Gross profit

Cost of sales refers to the cost of providing the goods and services sold during a period. It does not refer to the cost of goods and services bought. This is because the profit calculation insists that we only include the costs incurred to produce the current period's sales. If a clothes shop buys 500 suits during a period and sells 200, the cost of sales quoted would be the cost of the 200 suits sold (not the 500 suits bought). This concept is readily applicable in businesses that manufacture or trade in stock, where it is sometimes referred to by the alternative title of 'cost of goods sold.' Where a business sells a service, cost of sales would refer to the direct costs of providing that service. For example, in a hairdressing salon cost of sales would include the hairdressers' salaries along with consumables such as shampoo and conditioner. This brings us to our first profit figure.

Gross profit is the profit made on the basic trading activities of buying and selling goods and services. In the world of finance the word 'gross' means before deduction, whereas 'net' means after deduction. Gross profit refers to the profit earned before deducting day-to-day operating costs. The income statement of Maykem & Sellem tells us that the company achieved sales of $200 million and spent $126 million providing the goods and services sold, leaving $74 million gross profit to pay for its operating costs.

Operating costs are the day-to-day running costs of the business. This would include expenses such as marketing, administration, information technology, finance, human resources, and property costs. Now for some bad news! As is becoming apparent, the income statement contains a fair amount of jargon. To further compound the issue, there is additional jargon when discussing operating costs in particular. This extra terminology has nothing to do with the content of the financial statement, but refers to how the figures are worked out.

The profit calculation examines the sales during a period and deducts the costs incurred to generate that period's sales. It follows that operating costs need to be moved from the period in which the expenditure takes place to the period in which the related sales take place. To achieve this, four techniques are commonly encountered in practice:

* **Prepayment**

  Sometimes costs are paid in advance. To satisfy the profit calculation, amounts paid in advance need to be moved to the periods to which they relate. This is known as a 'prepayment' adjustment. For example, a business may have to pay a three-year maintenance contract on its equipment in advance. Each year, operating costs should only include that proportion of the original sum paid that relates to the current period's sales.

* **Accrual**

  Sometimes costs are paid in arrears. To ensure that operating costs reflect expenditure relating to the current period's sales, we need to include an estimate of expenditure that relates to the current period but for which no invoice has yet been received. This is known as an 'accrual' adjustment. For example, if during a year a company has only received electricity bills for the first nine months, operating costs will need to include an estimate of the electricity bills anticipated for the last three months. This is because, although the expenditure may not take place until the following year, it is being incurred to produce the current year's sales.

* **Depreciation**

  When a fixed asset is acquired its useful life may span several years. In keeping with the requirements of the profit calculation, operating expenses should only include that amount of the initial purchase price that relates to the current period's sales. This is known as a 'depreciation' adjustment. If a company pays $12,000 for a piece of equipment that it believes will last six years, it will need to spread this cost over the life of the asset.

Various techniques can be used to achieve this.

* The most popular one is the 'straight-line method,' which spreads the cost evenly (which in this case would be $2,000 per annum).

* Another technique used for spreading the cost is the 'reducing-balance method,' which apportions the greater part of the original cost to the early years of ownership. This tends to be appropriate for items deemed to lose value faster early in their life, such as vehicles.

* A third technique is the 'machine-hour method,' which apportions the original cost according to usage of the asset during a year. This is sometimes encountered when dealing with manufacturing equipment where an asset's life tends to be determined by usage rather than age.

It is worth noting another term that can be encountered when talking about depreciation: 'amortization.' In reality these two terms are totally interchangeable – they mean the same thing. However, some companies apply a subtle distinction whereby they refer to depreciation when dealing with tangible assets (assets that have a physical form) and amortization when dealing with intangible assets (assets that have no physical form). Such companies would refer to depreciation of furniture, but amortization of a lease on a property.

* **Provision for bad debts**
Customers who purchase goods and services on credit may fail to settle their debt in the future. To be consistent with the profit calculation, we need to include an allowance for accounts receivable arising in the current period that are expected to default in the future. This adjustment is known as a 'provision for bad debts.' If at the end of a year a company is owed $80,000 for sales that took place during the previous 12 months, out of which $2,000 is expected never to be paid, an allowance should be included within operating expenses for these potential bad debts. This is because these future bad debts will be a direct consequence of the sales that have taken place during the current year.

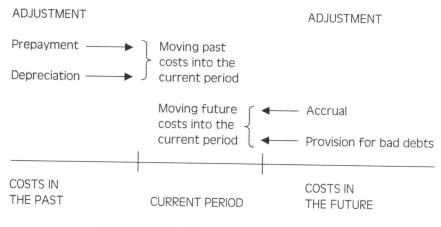

OPERATING COSTS – TIMING ADJUSTMENTS

What we are looking at here are timing adjustments. In other words, we are moving expenditure from one time period to another.

Prepayment and depreciation adjustments both charge against the current period costs that have already been incurred. Accrual and provision for bad debt adjustments do precisely the reverse: they charge against the current period costs that are going to arise in the future.

The bare bones
There are four main types of adjustment used to move operating costs from the period in which they are incurred to the period to which they relate:
- ✳ **Prepayment**
- ✳ **Accrual**
- ✳ **Depreciation**
- ✳ **Provision for bad debts**

We have now worked our way through the first two sections of the income statement. In the case of Maykem & Sellem, we see that the company generated sales during the year of $200 million, out of which $126 million was spent on goods and services sold, providing a gross profit of $74 million. Out of this $74 million, a further $54 million was spent on operating costs. This brings us to the second profit measure usually encountered in the income statement.

Operating profit is the term often applied to the profit achieved after paying for all the costs incurred in running the business. Other titles encountered include 'trading profit,' 'PBIT' (profit before interest and tax), and 'EBIT' (earnings before interest and tax). After paying its operating costs, Maykem & Sellem has produced an operating profit of $20 million. This can be regarded as the profit that management has produced, since every figure down to this line can be directly influenced by managers. The remainder of the income statement examines how this profit is to be distributed. In this respect, there are three parties who potentially want payment:

* **Providers of loan finance**
  who want to be paid interest on the funds provided
* **The government**
  who wants to charge tax on the profits achieved
* **The shareholders**
  who want a return on their investment

This explains why the final section of this document introduces three more deductions:

* **Interest payable**
* **Tax**
* **Dividends**

It also introduces three more profit definitions:

* **Profit before tax**
* **Profit after tax**
* **Retained profit**

Let's work down the remainder of the income statement line by line.

Interest payable is the interest due on funds borrowed. This has to be paid regardless of how much profit has been made. Note that the wording is 'interest payable,' not 'interest paid.' This is to ensure consistency with the profit calculation, which requires the amount chargeable to a period to be the interest that relates to producing that period's sales. We do not quote the actual interest paid, as this may relate to other periods. This can be viewed as the return on one source of finance: the return on borrowed funds. Examining the income statement for Maykem & Sellem it can be seen that, out of the $20 million operating profit, $2 million was payable in the form of interest. This brings us on to another definition of profit.

Profit before tax is the profit that has been made after paying a return to the providers of loan finance, but before paying a return to the shareholders. Unfortunately for shareholders, before arriving at the profit they are entitled to there is still one more distribution to go.

Tax, when mentioned in an income statement, usually refers to a very specific tax: that payable on profits. This should not be confused with other forms of taxation such as value added tax or sales tax. In the case of Maykem & Sellem, out of a profit before tax of $18 million, $6 million is payable to the government. This brings us to yet another profit definition.

Profit after tax is the critical figure from a shareholder's point of view, as this is the profit available exclusively for them. It is also sometimes referred to as 'net profit' or 'net income.' The company has paid all its expenses, paid interest on funds borrowed, and paid tax to the government. In the case of Maykem & Sellem, after paying tax of $6 million there is $12 million remaining for shareholders. They have two options for what to do with this money:

* **They can withdraw it**
* **They can reinvest it**

Both of these options are reported in the income statement, as dividends and as retained profit.

The bare bones
From the shareholders' perspective, profit after tax is the most important figure reported in an income statement, as it represents the total profit the business has made for them.

Dividends are payments of profit to shareholders. There is no rule that says how much profit should be paid out and how much should be reinvested. One piece of logic runs as follows:

* Pay low dividends when business is buoyant, so that profit can be reinvested to take advantage of the opportunities to grow profit rapidly in the future
* Pay high dividends when trading is tough as few (if any) opportunities may exist to reinvest the funds effectively

Although this has considerable intuitive appeal, alternative approaches are adopted. For example, some companies strive for steady dividend growth to provide their shareholders with a reliable source of income.

Maykem & Sellem's income statement tells us that out of $12 million profit available to shareholders, dividends of $4 million have been declared, leaving the bulk of the profit available for reinvestment. This leads us on to the final profit definition.

Retained profit is what is left over after dividends have been paid. This is profit being reinvested back into the business, which should result, hopefully, in increased profit in the future. In Maykem & Sellem's case, $8 million is reinvested back into the business.

Having worked your way through the income statement, bear in mind, from a shareholder's point of view, that the most important figure is the profit after tax. This tells a shareholder what has happened to their wealth. If a profit is declared at this level their wealth is going up, whereas if a loss is reported their wealth is going down. By studying this financial statement, the shareholders of Maykem & Sellem can see that their wealth has gone up by $12 million.

What does a cash flow statement tell you?

If a business is to survive, generating profit on its own is not enough – the business also needs cash flow. The cash flow statement tells us what is happening to cash within a business. It achieves this by looking at cash received during a period, deducting cash paid out, and thereby identifying how much cash remains.

The bare bones
A cash flow statement explains why cash balances change, by examining the cash receipts and the cash payments during a period.

A typical cash flow statement might be presented as shown below. As with the two previous financial statements, it is far easier to understand this statement if we break it down into sections (see overleaf).

MAYKEM & SELLEM INC.
CASH FLOW STATEMENT
FOR THE YEAR ENDED 31 DECEMBER

	$ million
Cash receipts	251
LESS Cash payments	−247
NET CASH FLOW	4
PLUS Opening cash balance	2
CLOSING CASH BALANCE	6

CASH FLOW STATEMENT – THE INITIAL VIEW

A cash flow statement is similar to your personal bank statement. It answers three questions:

* What has happened to cash during the period?
* How much cash was there at the start of the period?
* How much cash is there at the end of the period?

In order to answer the first of these questions, three figures need to be identified:

* Cash receipts
* Cash payments
* Net cash flow

MAYKEM & SELLEM INC.
CASH FLOW STATEMENT
FOR THE YEAR ENDED 31 DECEMBER

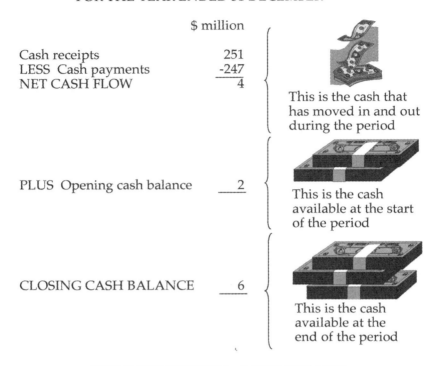

	$ million
Cash receipts	251
LESS Cash payments	-247
NET CASH FLOW	4

This is the cash that has moved in and out during the period

PLUS Opening cash balance	2

This is the cash available at the start of the period

CLOSING CASH BALANCE	6

This is the cash available at the end of the period

CASH FLOW STATEMENT – A SIMPLIFIED VIEW

Cash receipts is the total value of cash that has moved into the business during the period. Sources of cash receipts would include payments received from customers, loans received from banks, and cash received from shareholders in return for shares.

Cash payments is the total value of cash that has moved out of the business during the period. This would include payments to suppliers, payments to staff, payments for rent, repayments of loans, payments of tax, and dividends paid to shareholders.

Net cash flow tells us by how much the cash receipts exceeded the cash payments during the period or, if it has a negative value, by how much the payments exceeded the receipts. It is calculated by deducting total cash payments from total cash receipts.

According to the cash flow statement of Maykem & Sellem, the company received $251 million during the year, out of which it spent

$247 million, leaving a net cash inflow of $4 million.

Opening cash balance is the value of cash in the business at the start of the period. Maykem & Sellem started off the year with $2 million.

Closing cash balance tells you how much cash there is at the end of the period. This is calculated by taking the opening cash balance and adding on the net cash flow (or deducting the net cash flow if it has a negative value). Maykem & Sellem started off the year with $2 million and during the next 12 months receipts exceeded payments by $4 million, leaving the company with $6 million cash at the end of the year.

Given that healthy cash flow is a prerequisite for business survival, it may surprise you to hear that most companies do not devote a lot of time to analyzing their cash flow statement. When you receive a bank statement, your main preoccupation is making sure you have enough cash available to pay your bills. So it is in the business world. Businesses use cash flow statements to ensure that they can meet their financial commitments. The main reason this document does not tend to be subjected to rigorous analysis is that we have already been introduced to a financial statement that tells us where all the cash is currently invested – the balance sheet. This latter document tells us how much cash is tied up in property, equipment, inventory, and so forth. As a result, it is the balance sheet that most companies use to manage their cash, with the cash flow statement being used primarily to ensure that adequate cash exists within a business on a day-to-day basis.

Where do accounting scandals come from?

When producing their financial statements, most businesses endeavor to provide a realistic and objective view of their trading results. Regrettably, there will always be the occasional rogue business that tries to abuse the system, although fortunately these tend to be the exception rather than the rule. Even so, it is still worth having an appreciation of how such abuses can arise.

Many of the accounting scandals reported in the news originate from the fact that profit and cash flow are not the same thing. In most instances it is a relatively straightforward matter to confirm the cash flows in and out of a business. Profit is more problematic because it is concerned with wealth measurement, which is not so easy to verify.

Suppose you are trying to work out your own wealth by constructing a personal balance sheet. You are going to add up your assets and deduct your liabilities. One of your assets is a top-of-the-range music system. This forms part of your wealth and, as such, needs to be valued. Unfortunately, there are a variety of values you can choose from:

* **What you paid for it**
* **What you paid for it less an allowance for wear and tear**
* **What you could sell it for now**
* **What it would cost to replace it**

Each value has its own merits and the one you choose will ultimately affect your declared wealth. Businesses face the same dilemma. They must select a method for valuing their assets that they believe to be the most appropriate to their circumstances. This immediately suggests one method a business could use to enhance its value as reported in the balance sheet:

* **Overvalue existing assets**

Other methods also exist:

* **Create fictitious assets**
* **Undervalue known liabilities**
* **Omit known liabilities**

Consequently, never view a balance sheet as a statement of fact. It is a statement of wealth that must, by its very nature, be based on assumptions. As a result, it is common practice when companies report their results to investors, or to the public at large, also to provide notes to the statements detailing the various assumptions being made.

The income statement can also be manipulated, because it deals with changes in wealth. Manipulations within this document tend to be centered on the profit calculation, where

Profit in a period = Sales in a period
LESS Costs incurred to produce that
period's sales

This suggests two methods for manipulating reported profit:

* **Overstate sales**
* **Understate costs**

Bear in mind that the figures used in the profit calculation do not necessarily reflect cash received or cash paid out. Earlier in this chapter we looked at depreciation, where the purchase price of a fixed asset is spread over its useful life, in order to match the cost of the asset to the appropriate sales figure. For example, if a company buys some equipment for $1 million, which it estimates will have a useful life of five years, this results in an annual depreciation charge (assuming the cost is to be spread evenly) of $200,000 appearing in the income statement. Of course, if the company claims that the equipment will last for ten years, the annual depreciation charge falls to $100,000, thereby increasing annual profit. This illustrates just one of a variety of methods that could be used to manipulate reported sales and cost figures. Unfortunately, it is usually impossible to know the useful life of a fixed asset at the outset. All a company can do, therefore, is report an annual depreciation charge based on what it deems to be a realistic life expectation.

The bare bones

Many accounting scandals emanate from the ability to manipulate values in the balance sheet and the income statement.

To avoid abuses taking place, most companies have an annual audit. This involves auditors going into a company at the end of the trading year to verify that the financial statements are portraying a realistic view of the business. It should be noted that auditors are appointed by the shareholders and their role is to report to those share-holders on how they perceive the financial statements. The problem with the report the auditors produce is that they can never confirm that the accounts are correct. This is because (as we saw with your music system) there is no definitive method for measuring wealth. What the auditors will confirm is that the valuations that appear in the balance sheet and the changes in wealth declared in the income statement seem fair, given the circumstances of the company.

As a result, whenever studying the trading results of a business, it is always good practice to examine any accompanying notes regarding the assumptions being made. An unrealistic assumption could adversely affect the value of the business, both now and in the future. Even businesses that are very diligent in how they report their results can make assumptions that subsequently turn out to be wrong.

 The bare bones
The role of a company audit is to confirm to the share-holders that the trading results being reported are reasonable.

Stripping it down to basics...

There are three key financial statements in any business:

* **The balance sheet, which provides a statement of wealth**
* **The income statement, which determines whether the wealth of the business is going up or down**
* **The cash flow statement, which is used to confirm that there is adequate cash available**

These documents are required by a variety of groups to assess how the business is being managed. For example, they are used by shareholders to assess how their investment is performing and by man-agers to identify where action is required.

The balance sheet identifies what a business is worth by adding up what it owns and deducting what it owes. Most businesses divide what they own into two categories: fixed assets and current assets. They tend to divide what they owe into two categories as well: current liabilities and long-term liabilities. On this basis, the value of the shareholders' investment can be determined.

The income statement calculates changes in wealth by examining the sales for a period (regardless of whether cash for those sales has been received or not) and deducting the costs incurred to produce these sales. To achieve this, operating costs have to be moved from the period in which they are incurred to the period to which they relate and there are four main types of adjustment used to achieve this: prepayments, accruals, depreciation, and provisions for bad debts. Within this financial statement, the most important figure from a shareholder's perspective is profit after tax, as this represents the total profit available for their use.

Given that the income statement makes no reference to when cash is received or paid out, the cash flow statement is required to check that there is adequate cash available to meet expenses as they arise. It achieves this by examining the cash receipts and the cash payments that take place during a period.

Since the balance sheet and the income statement both look at wealth measurement, the figures contained within them can occasionally be subject to abuse. However, shareholders of companies endeavor to protect themselves from such abuses by appointing auditors to report back on the reliability of the trading results that the company has provided.

7 WHAT CAN YOU LEARN
FROM FINANCIAL STATEMENTS?

Your company's latest trading results have been released. The accompanying commentary highlights the main points: 'Sales have increased 8%. Operating profit has increased 12%. Profit after tax is up 11%. £30 million of debt finance has been successfully raised to finance a significant expansion of fixed assets. Cash generation has been improved through enhanced supplier terms and the company is maintaining sufficient cash balances to maximize its future flexibility.' Studying the financial statements confirms this is all true, but so what? What does this tell you about how the business is trading? It is one skill to be able to read financial statements. It is a different skill to understand what financial statements tell you about how a business is being managed.

In this chapter we are going to examine a method for analyzing financial statements that will enable you, in a matter of minutes, to develop a clear picture of how effectively the profit-making process is being managed.

What is the first thing you should look for?

In order to survive, companies need to produce a healthy rate of return on the funds invested by shareholders. This is the first issue that should be addressed when you're confronted with a set of financial statements. Return on equity tells you how effectively this is being done, where

$$\text{Return on equity} = \frac{\text{Profit}}{\text{Shareholders' funds}} \times 100\%$$

Profit is reported in the income statement, whereas shareholders' funds are reported in the balance sheet.

Reproduced below and overleaf are the balance sheet and income statement of Maykem & Sellem introduced in the previous chapter. The only difference in this instance is that the balance sheet contains figures for both the end of the current year and the end of the previous year.

MAYKEM & SELLEM INC.
BALANCE SHEET
AS AT 31 DECEMBER

	THIS YEAR $ million	LAST YEAR $ million
Fixed assets	78	70
Current assets	69	64
TOTAL ASSETS	147	134
LESS Current liabilities	−41	−40
Long-term liabilities	−22	−18
NET ASSETS	84	76
Capital	30	30
Reserves	54	46
SHAREHOLDERS' FUNDS	84	76

MAYKEM AND SELLEM – BALANCE SHEET

MAYKEM & SELLEM INC.
INCOME STATEMENT
FOR THE YEAR ENDED 31 DECEMBER

	THIS YEAR $ million
SALES	200
LESS Cost of sales	−126
GROSS PROFIT	74
LESS Operating costs	−54
OPERATING PROFIT	20
LESS Interest payable	−2
PROFIT BEFORE TAX	18
LESS Tax	−6
PROFIT AFTER TAX	12
LESS Dividends	−4
RETAINED PROFIT	8

MAYKEM AND SELLEM – INCOME STATEMENT

Before calculating the return on equity for this company, a couple of conventions need to be noted that are usually applied when combining information from the balance sheet and the income statement.

✳ **In the balance sheet, use average figures for the period**
A balance sheet is a statement of wealth at a point in time, typically the end of a trading period. Given that the values reported in this statement can change over time, it is normally recommended that average values be used. This can be achieved by extracting the value at the end of the period under review along with the value at the end of the previous period and then calculating an average of the two figures.

✳ **In the income statement, use the figures as shown**

An income statement summarizes trading during a period, not at a point in time. Consequently, the figures reported within this statement can be used as shown.

Let's apply these principles to the financial statements of Maykem & Sellem.

When calculating any performance measures using financial statements, the terminology used needs to be precise. For example, using the term 'profit' when looking at the income statement for Maykem and Sellem is not much use – there are five different lines that contain the term. We need to know which profit figure we are talking about. Here is a more definitive version of the return on equity calculation:

$$\text{Return on equity} = \frac{\text{Profit after tax}}{\text{Average shareholders' funds}} \times 100\%$$

We are going to look at profit after tax, because this is the total profit available to shareholders. In Maykem & Sellem's income statement, this figure was $12 million. We are going to use average shareholders' funds because this figure comes from the balance sheet and, for reasons already explained, an average value is more appropriate. Given that shareholders' funds in Maykem & Sellem were $84 million at the end of the current year and $76 million at the end of the previous year, this gives us average funds of $80 million. Based on these figures, we can identify the return on equity:

$$\text{ROE} = \frac{\text{Profit after tax of \$12 million}}{\text{Average shareholders' funds of \$80 million}} \times 100\%$$

$$= 15\%$$

On every $100 of shareholders' funds invested in the business, a profit of $15 has been generated.

The bare bones
The return on equity being achieved by a company can be established by combining shareholders' funds reported in the balance sheet with profit reported in the income statement.

What can financial statements tell you about how a business is being managed?

Having established the return on equity, the next logical step is to determine how this has been achieved. When looking at the profit-making process in Chapter 3, we noted that delivering a healthy return on equity can be broken down into three stages:

* Raising funds to finance assets
* Turning assets into sales
* Turning sales into profit

All the information needed to assess each of these stages can be obtained from the balance sheet and income statement.

The first stage in the profit-making process is to raise funds to finance assets. How this is achieved can be assessed in terms of gearing, where

$$\text{Gearing} = \frac{\text{Long-term borrowings}}{\text{Total long-term funds}} \times 100\%$$

As with return on equity, because we are dealing with financial statements, we need a more precisely defined calculation:

$$\text{Gearing} = \frac{\text{Average long-term liabilities}}{\text{Average shareholders' funds}} \times 100\%$$
$$\text{PLUS Average long-term liabilities}$$

Long-term liabilities represent amounts owed that are payable after one year. In the main, this can be viewed as long-term borrowing. Given that we are looking at the balance sheet, we need to use an average value. In the case of Maykem & Sellem, long-term liabilities at the end of the current year are $22 million compared with $18 million at the end of the previous year, providing an average value of $20 million. This needs to be divided by the total long-term funds invested in the business, which can be obtained from two possible sources: shareholders and in the form of long-term borrowing. Once again, because we are dealing with balance sheet values, averages ought to be used. We have already established that average shareholders' funds are $80 million, so we are in a position to calculate the gearing:

$$\text{Gearing} = \frac{\text{Average long-term liabilities of \$20 million}}{\substack{\text{Average shareholders' funds of \$80 million} \\ \text{PLUS} \\ \text{Average long-term liabilities of \$20 million}}} \times 100\%$$

$$= 20\%$$

Out of every $100 worth of long-term funds raised, $20 is borrowed. As explained in Chapter 3, the attraction of borrowing long-term funds is that it can potentially increase return on equity. Against this must be balanced the risk – if adequate sales are not achieved, return on equity might fall. Given that Maykem & Sellem is low geared (most long-term funds are raised from shareholders), it can be concluded that the company is reasonably low risk in terms of how it is financed.

The second stage of the profit-making process is to turn assets (which are funded by long-term funds) into sales, which can be assessed in terms of asset turnover:

$$\text{Asset turnover} = \frac{\text{Sales}}{\text{Total long-term funds}}$$

As before, when using financial statements a more precisely defined calculation is required:

$$\text{Asset turnover} = \frac{\text{Sales}}{\text{Average shareholders' funds}}$$
$$\text{PLUS Average long-term liabilities}$$

The sales figure is obtained from the income statement and, in the case of Maykem & Sellem, is $200 million. We have already established that average shareholders' funds are $80 million and average long-term liabilities are $20 million, which combined represent the total long-term funds raised. This is all the information we need to calculate asset turnover:

$$\text{Asset turnover} = \frac{\text{Sales of \$200 million}}{\begin{array}{c}\text{Average shareholders' funds of \$80 million}\\\text{PLUS}\\\text{Average long-term liabilities of \$20 million}\end{array}}$$

$$= 2$$

From every $1 invested in assets, $2 worth of sales have been produced during the year.

We can now move on to the third stage of the profit-making process: turning sales into profit. How effectively this is being done can be assessed in terms of profit margin:

$$\text{Profit margin} = \frac{\text{Profit}}{\text{Sales}} \times 100\%$$

Once again, to extract the appropriate figures from the financial statements, we need a more precise version of the calculation:

$$\text{Profit margin} = \frac{\text{Profit after tax}}{\text{Sales}} \times 100\%$$

Both of these figures are obtained from the income statement, so no averaging is required. In the case of Maykem & Sellem, sales are $200 million and profit after tax is $12 million, providing the following profit margin:

$$\text{Profit margin} = \frac{\text{Profit after tax of } \$12 \text{ million}}{\text{Sales of } \$200 \text{ million}} \times 100\%$$

$$= 6\%$$

By combining gearing, asset turnover, and profit margin, we can establish how the company achieved a return on equity of 15%. The easiest way to do this is to follow through what happens to each $100 worth of long-term funds raised.

✳ A **gearing** of 20% tells us that, to finance $100 of assets, $20 is raised in the form of long-term borrowings

So, to finance $100 worth of assets, shareholders only have to invest $80.

✳ An **asset turnover** of 2 tells us that from every $1 worth of assets, $2 worth of sales are generated during the year

If funds have been raised to finance $100 worth of assets, it follows that $200 worth of sales will be produced.

✳ A **profit margin** of 6% tells us that from $100 worth of sales, $6 profit is made

Having raised $100 to finance assets, which in turn have produced $200 worth of sales, the profit margin tells us that 6% of this latter figure will be profit; that is, $12.

Our analysis has shown that, at the outset, shareholders needed to invest $80 in order to finance each $100 worth of assets. We have followed through the profit-making process and established how this has resulted in $12 profit being produced. Given that $12 works out at 15% of $80, this explains how Maykem & Sellem generated a return on equity of 15%. Examining what happens to $100 worth of funds raised provides an intuitive method for analyzing the results of any business (see opposite).

The figures we have worked out become particularly powerful when comparisons are made. Two common comparisons encountered in practice are as follows:

* **Comparison with previous year**
  This highlights where performance is improving and/or deteriorating.
* **Comparison with similar businesses**
  This highlights competitive strengths and/or weaknesses.

 The bare bones
Financial statements contain all the information required to assess how effectively the profit-making process is being managed within a business.

It is worth noting that all of the analysis so far has been performed by extracting just four figures from financial statements:

FIGURE	SOURCE
Average shareholders' funds	Balance sheet
Average long-term liabilities	Balance sheet
Sales	Income statement
Profit after tax	Income statement

This demonstrates how, using very few figures, we can learn a lot about how a business is being run. Of course, financial statements contain a lot more information in addition to the four figures we have used. Consequently, considerable scope exists for delving deeper into

Gearing of 20% tells us that,
out of each $100 of long-term funds raised,
$80 is raised in the form of shareholders' funds and
$20 is raised in the form of long-term borrowing

which finances $100 of assets

Asset turnover of 2 tells us that,
from every $1 of assets, $2 of sales are produced

which provides $200 sales
($100 assets multiplied by 2)

Profit margin of 6% tells us that,
from every $100 sale, $6 profit is produced

which provides $12 profit
($200 sales multiplied by 6%)

which provides
RETURN ON EQUITY of 15%
($12 profit divided by $80 shareholders' funds)

A STRUCTURED APPROACH TO ANALYZING TRADING RESULTS

these documents to learn more about the management of the business, should the urge take us. Given there are entire texts dedicated to this subject, we will not go into it in any more depth here. Notwithstanding this, just performing the analysis we have carried out so far provides a lot of valuable information and also provides a basic framework for assessing how any business is being managed.

How do financial statements interrelate?

Having identified where the information comes from to assess each stage of the profit-making process, the function of each financial statement can be clarified.

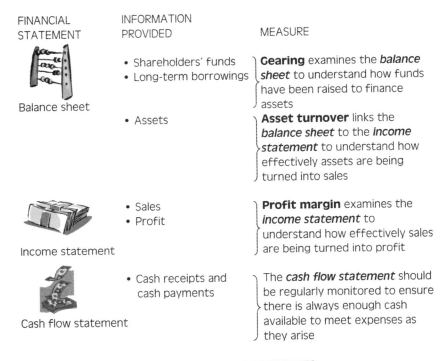

FINANCIAL STATEMENT	INFORMATION PROVIDED	MEASURE
Balance sheet	• Shareholders' funds • Long-term borrowings	**Gearing** examines the *balance sheet* to understand how funds have been raised to finance assets
	• Assets	**Asset turnover** links the *balance sheet* to the *income statement* to understand how effectively assets are being turned into sales
Income statement	• Sales • Profit	**Profit margin** examines the *income statement* to understand how effectively sales are being turned into profit
Cash flow statement	• Cash receipts and cash payments	The *cash flow statement* should be regularly monitored to ensure there is always enough cash available to meet expenses as they arise

USING FINANCIAL STATEMENTS

By combining the information contained within financial statements, we are able to assess how effective a company is at generating a return for its shareholders.

✳ **Return on equity**
    can be established by combining shareholders' funds in the **balance sheet** with profit reported in the **income statement**
✳ **Gearing**
    can be established by combining long-term borrowings in the **balance sheet** with shareholders' funds in the **balance sheet**

* **Asset turnover**
  can be established by combining long-term funds in the **balance sheet** with sales in the **income statement**
* **Profit margin**
  can be established by combining sales in the **income statement** with profit in the **income statement**
* **Cash flow**
  can be established by combining cash receipts and cash payments in the **cash flow statement**

The bare bones

The balance sheet, income statement, and cash flow statement must be continually monitored and analyzed if a business is to deliver a healthy return on equity.

How can financial statements be used to help manage a business?

Not only can financial statements tell us a how a company is progressing, they can also provide information that management can use to enhance the return to shareholders in the future.

* **Balance sheet**
  The balance sheet provides information on two issues that can have a dramatic impact on the need for shareholders' funds:

  ☆ It shows how funds have been invested in assets
  ☆ It shows how funds have been raised

Management should use this information to keep assets to a minimum (but without jeopardizing sales), thus keeping the need for shareholders' funds to a minimum. Also, gearing should be maintained at appropriate levels to provide a reasonable return to shareholders, while not exposing the company to unnecessary risk.

✳ **Income statement**
The income statement provides information on two further issues that can have a dramatic impact on the profit achieved:

☆ It shows the sales generated
☆ It shows the costs incurred

Management should combine these two pieces of information to ensure that the costs being incurred are appropriate to the level of sales being achieved, in order to maximize the opportunities available for producing profit.

✳ **Cash flow statement**
The cash flow statement provides a piece of information that is critical to business survival:

☆ It shows the cash available to pay expenses

By producing cash flow statements on a regular basis (many companies prepare them daily), management can ensure that cash is always available to meet expenditure commitments.

To summarize, using the balance sheet to minimize the need for shareholders' funds, while using the income statement to maximize the profitability of sales achieved, should result in a healthy return on equity. In addition, a cash flow statement should be regularly consulted to confirm that there is always enough cash available.

The bare bones
Financial statements provide information that can help management improve return on equity in the future.

What are the danger signals to watch out for?

A potent use of financial statements is to provide information about issues that might adversely affect trading performance in the future. This can most readily be achieved by studying trends from one year to the next. Clearly, a deterioration in return on equity will concern investors, but on its own it does not tell us why this is happening or if future trading is being put in jeopardy. Trends in gearing, asset turnover, and profit margin are far more useful in this respect.

Is there an increase in gearing?

Increases in gearing could potentially improve return on equity. However, this must be viewed in the context of the potential risks.

* **What is the 'interest cover'?**
  This is calculated from the income statement, by dividing operating profit by interest payable. In the case of Maykem & Sellem, operating profit is $20 million and interest payable is $2 million, providing an interest cover of 10. This tells us that the company is earning ten times more profit than the interest currently being paid. The higher this figure, the less chance there is of the company being unable to meet its future interest commitments.
* **What is the sales growth from one year to the next?**
  Weak sales growth could lead to deteriorating profits for investors if interest payments are increasing.

Is there a decrease in asset turnover?

Falling asset turnover is often a precursor to cash flow problems.

* **What is happening to fixed assets as a percentage of sales?**
* **What is happening to current assets as a percentage of sales?**

Either of these percentages increasing tends to be the first indicator of assets becoming less productive. If cash is being unnecessarily tied up in assets, this could affect the company's ability to generate cash in the future.

Is there a decrease in profit margin?

Falling profit margins are usually indicative of cost management issues.

✳ **What is happening to gross profit as a percentage of sales?**
When this percentage is falling, it often indicates increased competition and/or problems with the product offer.
✳ **What is happening to operating costs as a percentage of sales?**
When this percentage is increasing, it often indicates poor cost control.

If one or more of these trends is identified, management should take appropriate action to address these issues before they adversely affect long-term trading performance.

Stripping it down to basics...

By combining the information contained in financial statements, how effective a company is at providing a return for its shareholders can be readily assessed. In addition, financial statements can be used to help management identify action required to deliver a healthy return in the future. Also, by examining trends, potential future trading problems can be identified and addressed before they adversely affect long-term trading performance.

8 WHAT CAN YOU LEARN FROM THE FINANCIAL PRESS?

Every so often you have a go. You pick up the newspaper and turn to the financial pages. All you see are endless columns of figures. None of it makes any sense. The only thing you have managed to ascertain is that shares in your company are currently trading at $14.28, well below the $30 price they were commanding a year ago. Nothing seems to have changed significantly – same products, same factories, same customers, and even the same coffee machine at the end of the corridor. However, word throughout the business is that in response to the falling share price, there are going to be 'significant changes in the corporate operational model.' As far as you are concerned this is just a rather grandiose way of saying that staff cutbacks are imminent. Having talked to several of your colleagues, it would appear that none of them has any real understanding of share prices or why they move. The only thing they are certain about is that when the share price drops all hell breaks loose!

As you will discover, share prices do not reflect current trading. When you look at information about them you are looking into the future. This information is our financial crystal ball. Being able to look into the future can provide enormous benefits:

* You can assess the prospects of your own company
* You can assess the prospects of your competitors
* You can assess the prospects of your industry

If you understand the principles that enhance the share price of companies quoted on a public stock exchange, exactly the same concepts can be employed to increase the value of a privately owned company. There is no doubt about it: understanding share prices and why they move is a useful skill set for every manager.

Although the financial press contains information about all sorts of markets such as bonds, currencies, commodities, and so forth, it is  share prices that tend to be of concern to management. **In this chapter we are going to examine share prices, why they move, and how this information can be used to assess the future trading prospects of any business.**

THE FINANCIAL PRESS – A CORPORATE CRYSTAL BALL

How do you value a company?

The balance sheet of a company, discussed in Chapter 6, gives the value of shareholders' funds by adding up what a company owns (its assets) and deducting what a company owes (its liabilities). This is called the 'book value':

Book value = Total assets – Total liabilities
            = Shareholders' funds (as stated in the balance sheet)

If the Max Spending Corporation has $250 million worth of assets and $175 million worth of liabilities, the shareholders own the difference: $75 million. This can be viewed as the value of funds that shareholders have physically invested in the business. Another way of interpreting this is that, in theory at least, the shareholders of the Max Spending Corporation could close the company down tomorrow, sell everything the business owns, pay off everything it owes, and walk away with $75 million.

The bare bones
The book value of a business is the value of shareholders' funds as stated in the balance sheet.

Book value is not the only method for valuing the shareholders' investment. An alternative method is called 'market value' and is calculated as follows:

Market value = Number of shares in issue x Market price per share

If the Max Spending Corporation has 5 million shares in issue that are currently valued at $25 each, the market value would be as follows:

Market value = 5 million shares x $25 per share
= $125 million

This is the value that investors currently place on the company. In other words, based on the current share price, if somebody wanted to buy the company right now they would need to pay $125 million for it. This is very different from the book value of $75 million.

The bare bones
The market value of a company is defined as:
   Number of shares in issue
   multiplied by the share price

Why would anyone be willing to pay more than the value of the business as stated in the balance sheet? If the business is indeed bought for $125 million, the first $75 million of this is being paid for the shareholders' funds as stated in the balance sheet. Given that shareholders' funds are tied up in assets, it follows that this $75 million is being paid to acquire the company's assets such as property, equipment, inventory, and so on. So what is the remaining $50 million buying?

The difference between the market value of a business and its book value is called goodwill:

Goodwill = Market value – Book value

Many differing claims are made about what goodwill represents. Some people regard it as a payment for the reputation of the business, others claim it is a payment for the customer base, while others claim it is a payment for the brand name – the list goes on. In reality, good-will is a payment for something very specific: it is a payment for future profits. If future profits are expected to be high, investors will be willing to pay a large premium to get their hands on this income stream. Of course, if future profits are expected to be low, so too will be the premium that investors are prepared to pay.

 The bare bones
Goodwill is the premium that investors are prepared to pay, over the book value of a company, in order to acquire its future profits.

THE RELATIONSHIP BETWEEN BOOK VALUE AND MARKET VALUE

The critical point to note is that market value is influenced by expectations of future profit performance. This means that to increase the market value, it is not necessary to deliver high profits right now. What is required is a management strategy that investors believe will deliver healthy profits in the future.

What determines share prices?

The market value of a company (also known as its 'market capi-talization') is calculated by multiplying together two figures:

* The number of shares in issue
* The market price per share

The number of shares in issue is up to the company. What is far more important is the amount of money it wants to raise. For example, suppose the Gassy Beer Company wants to raise $10 million. There are many ways in which this can be done:

* It could issue 10 million shares at $1 each
* It could issue 5 million shares at $2 each
* It could issue 2 million shares at $5 each

and so the options continue.

It is entirely up to the company which option it selects. There is an argument, though, that the higher the price of a share the less trad-able it becomes. For example, if the Gassy Beer Company decides to issue just two shares at $5 million each, there probably would not be very many potential buyers! As a result, most companies like to keep their share prices reasonably low in order to encourage trading.

Of course, once the shares have been issued, the market value of the company will be dependent on the price that investors are subse-quently willing to pay for those shares, which will be driven by expec-tations of future profits. If information comes to light that suggests the company will make higher profits in the future than previously expected, the value of goodwill will increase and this will be reflected in an increased share price. Conversely, if information becomes avail-able that suggests that profits in the future will be lower than previ-ously expected, the value of goodwill will decrease, and this will be reflected in a reduced share price.

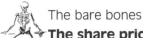

The bare bones
The share price of a company is influenced by expectations of future profit performance.

Before going any further, it is important to establish what type of company we are talking about when examining share prices. Broadly speaking, companies can be divided into two categories:

* **Publicly quoted companies**
  Companies that are quoted on a public stock exchange such as New York, London, or Tokyo.
* **Privately owned companies**
  Companies that are not quoted on a public stock exchange.

How the share price is established depends on which sort of company we are dealing with.

Let's start by looking at publicly quoted companies. If a company wants to raise a lot of capital – maybe millions of dollars – the most effective way of doing this is to offer shares to the public at large. In this situation, potential investors (who will not tend to have an intimate knowledge of the company concerned) will only want to invest if they have the option of readily selling their shares should they so wish. To facilitate this, companies need to obtain what is called a 'listing' on a stock exchange. This is a market where buyers and sellers of shares come together to trade. Such a market has two distinct advantages:

* **Shareholders can monitor the price of their shares on a daily basis**
* **Shareholders can readily buy and sell shares whenever they wish**

Shareholders of a privately owned company are usually few in number and are not able to sell their shares to the public, as they are not quoted on a public stock exchange. A family-owned company is typical of the sort of business that falls into this category. Shares can only be transferred by private treaty and restrictions may exist regarding to whom shares may be transferred (e.g. approval of the directors might be required). As a result, share transfers in such companies tend to be a fairly rare occurrence. Also, since there is no recognized market for trading the shares, it is often difficult to agree a share price – it is literally down to the negotiating skills of the parties concerned. However, as we will discover, methods do exist for estimating the value of such shares. This form of company tends to be associated with businesses that do not need to raise large amounts of capital.

Whether a company is publicly quoted or privately owned affects how the share price is determined:

* **Publicly quoted**
  Share prices are quoted on a public stock exchange.
* **Privately owned**
  Share prices have to be estimated based on available information. This demands an ability to use share valuation techniques.

Although the approaches may differ, the principles underpinning the valuation of both types of entity are very similar. Indeed, if you are able to interpret the share price information of publicly quoted companies as reported in the financial press, you already have the skill set to value the shares of a privately owned company.

How can you interpret the share price information of a publicly quoted company?

The share prices of publicly quoted companies are listed in the financial press; that is, any newspaper that provides detailed share price information on a daily basis. This is our crystal ball: it provides us with a glimpse of what we can expect in the future. It must be emphasized that we are dealing with expectations here, and expectations can be wrong. Provided that you bear this in mind, the financial press can prove to be a potent source of information. Used carefully, it can help us formulate trading expectations of individual companies, industries, and even entire economies.

The bare bones
The financial press provides information on how the share prices of publicly quoted companies are performing.

When looking at company data in the financial press, it tends to be presented in tabular form and looks much the same regardless of the stock exchange being reported. Typical information you are likely to encounter for an individual company is as follows:

Company	Price	Change	52 week High	Low	Yield	P/E
	$	$	$	$	%	
Max Spending	25.00	+0.21	25.18	16.37	3.2	17.8

TYPICAL LAYOUT OF COMPANY DATA

This can look daunting to the uninitiated, but is easier to grasp if we appreciate that the information comprises just three elements:

* **Share price information**
* **Dividend information**
* **Profit information**

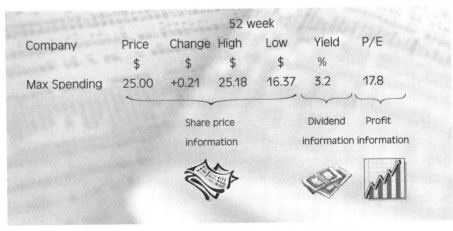

COMPANY DATA COMPRISES THREE ELEMENTS

Share prices are set by supply and demand. If lots of people want to sell shares (suggesting they are pessimistic about the company's prospects) but very few people want to buy, the share price will fall. You can witness the same phenomenon in a shop. If merchandise is not selling it will be marked down to a lower price to encourage people to buy. The reverse is true when lots of people want to buy shares (suggesting they are optimistic about the company's prospects) but very few people want to sell: the share price will increase.

Share price information in the financial press comments on this activity. Four figures are commonly quoted in this respect:

* **Price**
* **Change**
* **52 week high**
* **52 week low**

Price refers to the price of a single share at the close of business on the previous trading day. In this instance, Max Spending has a share price of $25.00.

Change usually refers to the change in the price of a single share over the preceding 24-hour trading period. Max Spending's share price of $25.00 represents an increase of $0.21 on the previous day. From a shareholder's point of view, this is an important figure because it indicates whether the current value of the share is increasing or decreasing. What shareholders like to see is regular increases.

52 week high tells us the highest price the shares have attained in the previous 52 weeks. Max Spending's shares have traded as high as $25.18. Some investors use a rule of thumb regarding this figure, which runs as follows. If the share price is close to its 52 week high, this suggests that news must have broken recently that has enhanced expectations of future performance, thereby having a favorable effect on the share price. This appears to be the situation in the case of Max Spending, which currently has a share price of $25.00, close to its 52 week high of $25.18. Regrettably, this is only a rule of thumb and nobody has defined what is meant by the term 'close to,' so a certain amount of subjectivity is involved.

52 week low tells us the lowest price the shares have reached in the previous 52 weeks. Max Spending's shares have traded as low as $16.37. As in the case of the 52 week high statistic, there is a rule of thumb surrounding this figure. If the share price is close to its 52 week low, this suggests that news must have broken recently that has downgraded expectations of future performance, having an adverse effect on the share price. Once again, this is only a very loosely defined guideline.

The bare bones
Examining share prices relative to their high and low points during the preceding 52 weeks can provide an indication of how expectations are changing regarding future performance.

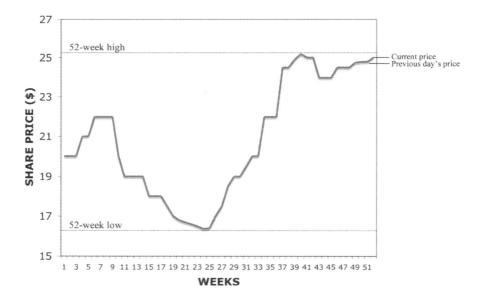

SHARE PRICE INFORMATION PROVIDED IN THE FINANCIAL PRESS

Despite what we have learned about share prices so far, don't rush off and read the financial press just yet! There is a serious problem about studying share prices in isolation. Clearly, if you have shares in a company you want to know if the value of your investment is going up or down. For this purpose the information examined so far is very useful. It is a different matter if you want to compare companies, however. If one company has a share price of $100 while another has a share price of $20, does it follow that the company with the higher share price is five times more successful than the company with the lower price?

We have already noted that it is up to companies how many shares they issue. If they issue a lot of shares, they will have a lower share price. If they issue very few shares, they will have a higher share price. Therefore, all we can surmise by comparing share prices is that one company may have fewer shares in issue than another and, based on the information examined so far, we cannot even be certain about that.

The bare bones
Share prices of different companies are not comparable as they are influenced by the number of shares in issue.

When comparing performance across companies, dividend information can prove to be more useful than share price information. In the financial press, dividend information is normally limited to 'yield.'

Yield (which is an abbreviation for 'dividend yield') evaluates a company's most recent annual dividend per share in relation to the current market price of the share:

$$\text{Dividend yield} = \frac{\text{Dividend per share}}{\text{Market price of share}} \times 100\%$$

If a company declared a dividend last year of $1.50 per share and the current price of its shares is $30.00, dividend yield would be as follows:

$$\text{Dividend yield} = \frac{\text{Dividend per share of }\$1.50}{\text{Market price of share of }\$30.00} \times 100\% = 5\%$$

If you bought shares in the company right now, based on the dividend declared last year, you could expect an annual return of 5% in the form of dividends. Max Spending has a dividend yield of 3.2%, which tells you that for every $100 invested in shares at the current price, you can expect an annual dividend of $3.20 if dividends remain unchanged.

Although yield only comments on profits being paid out by a company – it does not comment on profits being reinvested – it is often used as an indicator of how a company may be expected to do in the future. This is based on the premise that companies will be keen to reinvest profits when there is a buoyant market with ample opportunities to invest funds effectively. Conversely, if investment opportunities are limited, companies will be more tempted to pay funds back to shareholders in the form of dividends. It follows that if a company has a high dividend yield (it is paying out high levels of dividend relative to its share price), this is usually taken to indicate low levels of reinvested profit, suggesting that management is cautious about the future. Conversely, if a company has a low dividend yield, this can be taken to indicate high levels of reinvested profit, suggesting that management must be optimistic about the future. Unfortunately, low dividends (or even no dividends at all) are also associated with poor profit performance or a cash flow crisis.

Let's summarize these conclusions:

* **High yield**
  Often associated with limited growth opportunities
* **Low yield**
  Either the company is optimistic about the future and is reinvesting heavily
  Or the company has poor profit performance
  Or the company has hit a cash flow crisis and is about to disappear into oblivion!

This suggests that using dividend yield on its own as an indicator of future performance is not to be recommended. It can be a useful indicator of a company's ability to provide income, but it does not tell you the whole story. It needs to be coupled with other information in order to build up an overall view of a company's trading prospects.

The bare bones
Dividend yield provides the percentage return that can be expected on shares in the form of dividends, based on payments in the previous year.

If you ask a shareholder what their main preoccupation is when buying shares, they will probably tell you it is future profitability. The assets of the company are important, but ultimately they are a means to an end. What counts above all else is future profits, as this will affect the price that is being paid for those shares and will also affect future dividend payments. In Chapter 4 we established that the main measure shareholders use to assess a company's ability to generate profit is earnings per share (EPS). This suggests that there must be a link between the price shareholders are willing to pay for a share and what they believe EPS will be in the future. If shareholders anticipate strong EPS performance, they will be prepared to pay a high price to obtain a share. If shareholders anticipate weak EPS performance, they will only pay a low price.

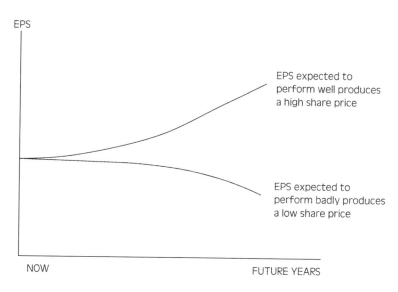

SHARE PRICES ARE DRIVEN BY ANTICIPATED EPS PERFORMANCE

Linking the price of a share to EPS produces the key measure of profit performance encountered in the financial press: the 'price–earnings ratio' (or P/E ratio).

The **P/E ratio** (also known as the 'earnings multiple' or the 'profits multiple') is usually regarded as the most powerful indicator of potential performance reported in the financial press. It examines the relationship between the current market price of a share and the company's latest reported EPS:

$$\text{P/E ratio} = \frac{\text{Market price per share}}{\text{Earnings per share}}$$

If a company's EPS last year was $0.50 and it currently has a share price of $10.00, the P/E ratio would be as follows:

$$\text{P/E ratio} = \frac{\text{Market price per share of } \$10.00}{\text{Earnings per share of } \$0.50} = 20$$

This tells us that investors are currently paying 20 times last year's EPS in order to obtain a share in this company. In other words, they are paying 20 times the profit. Shareholders in Max Spending are paying 17.8 times more than last year's EPS. How does this help us assess the prospects of the company?

If a company has a high P/E ratio when compared with other companies, this indicates that investors are paying far more than current profits in order to obtain the shares. To justify this, it follows that they must be expecting profits to perform well in the future. If a company has a low P/E ratio, again when compared against other companies, it follows that investors are expecting less impressive profit performance in the future.

This explains the popularity of this measure. First of all, it is directly comparable across companies. Also, unlike dividend yield (which only looks at the share price in relation to dividends paid), the P/E ratio looks at the share price in relation to total profits earned.

Let's summarize the conclusions that can be drawn when examining P/E ratios:

* **High P/E ratio**

  Investors are paying a high price for shares relative to current profit, suggesting expectations of healthy profit performance in the future.
* **Low P/E ratio**

  Investors are paying a low price for shares relative to current profit, suggesting expectations of poor profit performance in the future.

There are always exceptions to these conclusions. A company's profit might halve one year. If this is viewed as a temporary phenomenon subsequent profit forecasts will remain largely unaffected, resulting in a minimal impact on the share price. However, given that reported earnings per share will have halved, the P/E ratio will effectively double. Another factor that can have a significant impact on P/E ratios is risk. If a company is perceived as high risk investors will not be willing to pay a high price for a share, as there is a very real possibility of their investment falling in value. Conversely, if a company is perceived as low risk investors will be willing to pay more for its shares, as it is far less likely that the value of their investment will fall. As a general rule, the higher the risk attached to a company, the lower its share price will be, resulting in a lower P/E ratio.

The bare bones
The P/E ratio provides an indication of expected performance in future EPS.

P/E ratios provide a sanity check on a share price. Say you have just received a hot tip: 'Buy shares in the Wooden Saucepan Company: they're only $6 each.' On its own the share price does not tell you very much. Looking at the P/E ratio puts it in context. If the P/E ratio is 600, this means that the share price is 600 times current earnings per share. Future profits would need to grow dramatically in order to justify this sort of earnings multiple. You would be strongly advised to look in more depth at the company's trading prospects before parting with your cash. If the P/E ratio is 2, you are only paying two years' worth of profits to acquire the shares, which may lead you to believe that this is a good time to invest as the shares seem cheap. This does raise a question, however: why are they so cheap? Maybe investors are concerned about future trading prospects. Once again, look at the company in more depth before you part with your cash.

Below is a summary of what we have learned about interpreting the financial press.

Company	Price	Change	52 week High	Low	Yield	P/E
	$	$	$	$	%	
Max Spending	25.00	+0.21	25.18	16.37	3.2	17.8
	These figures are useful if you hold shares in this company and want to know how your investment is doing but they are not comparable across companies		These figures can be used to determine whether trading prospects have recently been upgraded or downgraded		This figure provides an indication of future dividend performance	This figure is the key indicator of anticipated future profit performance

INTERPRETING THE FINANCIAL PRESS

If there is one message you should extract from this discussion above all else, it is this: share prices are directly influenced by expectations of future performance and these expectations are continually being updated. This means that the share price information provided in the financial press is only as good as current investors' expectations. Investors can be wrong! Just because a company has a high P/E ratio does not guarantee it will do well in the future. All the ratio is telling you is that investors are prepared to pay far more than current profits to acquire shares in the company.

The bare bones
Share price volatility results from expectations of future profit performance being continually updated.

Given that share prices are driven by expectations of future performance, these expectations can be used for a variety of purposes:

✳ Assessing the trading prospects of your own company (if it is publicly quoted)
✳ Assessing the trading prospects of your competitors
✳ Assessing the trading prospects of your customers
✳ Assessing the trading prospects of your suppliers
✳ Assessing the trading prospects of your industry (which can be extremely useful when creating business plans)

How do you manage share prices?

As mentioned previously, if you want to increase the share price of your company you do not need to increase current profits. What you need is a strategy that will increase profits in the future. If you can convince shareholders that this strategy will succeed, the share price will follow. Consequently, share price volatility can be seen as emanating from two sources:

✳ Market factors such as interest rates, unemployment, and competition
✳ The ability of management to sell a convincing profit story

Market factors are usually outside a company's control, so a certain amount of share price movement should always be expected due to altering external circumstances. However, some share price volatility can be removed by developing a consistent strategy to make profit in the future in which the shareholders can have faith. This can be most effectively achieved by providing robust forecasts.

It is often suggested that the ideal strategy is to deliver results that are just above forecast. This indicates sound planning, while also providing a small bonus for shareholders at the end of the year. Being significantly below forecast is clearly not desirable. However, being significantly above forecast may also be viewed unfavorably if it is perceived as a sign of weak management control.

Ultimately, managing share prices is about building up share-holders' trust. For this to be achieved, managers at all levels need to develop realistic commercial plans that are subsequently fulfilled. In other words, it is about management control. Achieving this will help reduce some of the violent share price swings to which some companies can be prone. However, fluctuations will still exist and this must be accepted as part of being a publicly quoted company.

How do you determine the share price of a privately owned company?

The financial press provides share price information relating to publicly quoted companies. If you are looking at a privately owned company (one that is not quoted on a public stock exchange), how do you value the shares in this instance?

Probably the most common and straightforward technique used to value shares in a privately owned company is the 'earnings multiple method.' This builds on the principles introduced when studying the share price performance of publicly quoted companies. If a publicly quoted company has a P/E ratio of 15, this tells us that investors value the shares at 15 times the current earnings of those shares. The same principle can be applied to privately owned companies. The earnings multiple method estimates the value of a share by basing it on a multiple of current earnings, using the following formula:

Share price = Earnings per share x P/E ratio

To apply this technique we obviously need two pieces of information:

* **Earnings per share**
* **P/E ratio**

The earnings per share would typically be the last reported earnings per share for the company, which can be established from its annual report. However, alternatives are sometimes used. If profit performance has been inconsistent, an average of the last few years might be taken. If losses or unusually low profits are currently being experienced, an estimated future earnings per share may be used instead.

A P/E ratio can be estimated by studying the ratios of similar publicly quoted companies in the same industry. In this way an appropriate P/E ratio can be identified, adjusting for factors such as expected profit growth and risk. If a company is perceived as higher risk than its publicly quoted counterparts, a lower P/E ratio might be applied. If a company is perceived as potentially having far higher earnings growth than its publicly quoted counterparts, a higher P/E ratio might be deemed applicable.

The bare bones
Share prices of privately owned companies can be estimated using the earnings multiple method.

Let's look at a simple example. Growdough is a private company and its directors are considering applying for a quotation on a public stock exchange. They therefore need to place a value on the 2 million shares currently in issue. Being someone who is recognized as having a sound understanding of share prices, you are invited to advise them and you identify this as a perfect opportunity to apply the earnings multiple method.

You explain that the first step is to identify an earnings per share figure. Given that the company has seen consistent growth in earnings per share over the last few years, you deem it appropriate to use the latest reported figure of $0.75. You point out to the directors (who are already in awe of your financial acumen) that a P/E ratio is also required. You study share information for similar publicly quoted companies, noting that most seem to be in the range between 12 and 19. Having studied Growdough, you are convinced that its earnings prospects are stronger than many of its competitors, so you conclude that a P/E of 18 would be appropriate. This enables you to estimate the value of a Growdough share:

Share value   = Earnings per share of $0.75 × P/E ratio of 18
             = $13.50

Given that there are 2 million shares in issue, you take great pride in informing the directors that they have a company that, in your opinion, is worth approximately $27 million (2 million shares at $13.50 each). As a parting comment (and to firmly establish your guru-like status within the company), you point out that if the directors can develop a plan that will increase anticipated future profits further, this will enhance the P/E ratio, thereby further increasing the value of the company.

How do you value an unincorporated business?

The principles used to value the shares of a privately owned company can be adapted to value an unincorporated business, whether it be a sole trader or a partnership.

Suppose you own a restaurant. It has built up a loyal customer base and consistently produces profit. You now want to sell it, but need to determine what it is worth. There are no shares in existence and you own the premises.

At the outset, bear in mind you are selling a business, so what the purchaser is interested in is future profits. This makes the transaction identical to selling shares in a company. When shareholders buy shares in a company, they too are interested in future profits. This would suggest that a similar approach should be adopted, whether you are valuing a company or an unincorporated business.

Let's revisit how we valued the shares of Growdough above. The technique we used was the earnings multiple method, which values shares using the following formula:

Share price $=$ Earnings per share $\times$ P/E ratio

This tells us that the value of an individual share is a multiple of the profit that share is currently earning. In the case of Growdough, the P/E ratio we used was 18. In other words, each share is valued at 18 times the earnings of that share. It follows that the total value of the company must be 18 times the total earnings of the company. This provides us with a means for valuing any type of business:

Value of business = Total earnings x Profit multiple

As when valuing the shares of a company, the earnings would typically be the last reported earnings of the business, maybe substituting an average annual figure if profit performance has been inconsistent, or an estimated future profit figure if losses or unusually low profits are being experienced. The profit multiple can be estimated by studying the multiples for which similar businesses are being sold, adjusting for factors such as expected profit growth and risk.

Suppose your restaurant has seen solid profit growth over recent years, with a profit of $600,000 being reported for the last year. Similar businesses have been selling locally at about 10 times annual profit and you have no reason to believe your restaurant will be viewed differently. The selling price can now be established:

Value of business = Total earnings of $600,000 x Profit multiple of 10
= $6,000,000

The bare bones
Unincorporated businesses can be valued by applying a multiple (which is a reflection of future trading prospects) to the annual profit figure.

Stripping it down to basics...

There are two ways to value the shareholders' investment in a company:

* **The book value is the value of shareholders' funds as stated in the balance sheet**
* **The market value is the value of shareholders' funds as determined by the share price**

The difference between market value and book value is called goodwill, which represents the premium investors are prepared to pay in order to acquire future profits.

The share price of a company is influenced by expectations of future profit performance. When it comes to determining share prices, companies can be divided into two broad categories: publicly quoted and privately owned.

Share prices of publicly quoted companies can be ascertained from the financial press. Information provided can be divided into three elements:

* Share price information, which includes details of how prices have changed
* Dividend information, which is measured in terms of yield
* Profit information, which is measured in terms of the price–earnings ratio

Although share prices across companies are not comparable, examining them relative to their high and low points during the preceding 52 weeks can provide an indication of how expectations regarding the future performance of that company are changing. Yield provides the percentage return that can be expected on shares in the form of dividends, based on payments in the previous year. The price–earnings ratio provides an indication of expected future profit performance, by expressing the current share price as a multiple of the previous year's earnings per share. Share prices tend to be volatile, though, because expectations of future performance are being continually updated.

Share prices of privately owned companies can be estimated using techniques such as the earnings multiple method. This approach can also be readily adapted to provide a means for valuing unincorporated businesses.

9 HOW DO YOU KNOW IF A COMPANY IS BEING WELL MANAGED?

An email has just arrived in your inbox. It is the quarterly address from your company's chairman to the staff: 'The company has seen a period of sustained growth, with sales and profits strengthening each year. As you are no doubt aware, we have recently had a team of management consultants working with us to assist in developing our strategy for the future. The Board of Directors are now committed to focusing attention on creating shareholder value and this must be the focus of attention for all managers and staff within the organization. Everything we do must be seen to create value. We know we have the capability to deliver on this and we are confident each and every one of you will play your part. Good luck! Seymour Khash, Chairman.' You are bemused. What is shareholder value? Is it just another way of saying make more profit? If that's the case, why not just say so? It sounds like just another management fad. No doubt it will pass and in a few months' time everything will be back to normal.

Shareholder value is definitely not a fad and it's a concept that is relevant to most types of business. As such, managers should be aware of what it is and be continually trying to devise strategies to enhance it. **In this chapter we are going to see how shareholder value combines information in financial statements with information in the financial press to determine whether or not a company is a worthwhile investment.**

What is shareholder value?

The principle of shareholder value is easy to grasp – it simply refers to the value of the shareholders' investment. So when companies talk about creating shareholder value, they are talking about increasing the value of the shareholders' investment.

Although the concept is reasonably easy to grasp, determining whether or not companies are creating shareholder value is somewhat more involved.

 The bare bones
Creating shareholder value means increasing the value of the shareholders' investment.

How do you know if a company is creating shareholder value?

In the previous chapter we established that there are two ways to value a company: book value and market value. Suppose shareholders' funds, as reported in a company's balance sheet, total $10 million. This is its book value. If the market value is $12 million, it is evident that additional value of $2 million has been created in excess of the funds physically invested in the business. This premium, as we have seen, is called goodwill. However, simply measuring the value of goodwill in a business does not tell us how effective the management team are at creating it. If one company has goodwill valued at $200,000 while another company has goodwill valued at $7 million, does it follow that the latter company is more effective at creating shareholder value? It is impossible to say, as we might be comparing companies that vary greatly in size.

In order to assess how good management is at creating share-holder value a powerful measure has been developed called the 'market to book ratio':

$$\text{Market to book ratio} = \frac{\text{Market price per share}}{\text{Book value per share}}$$

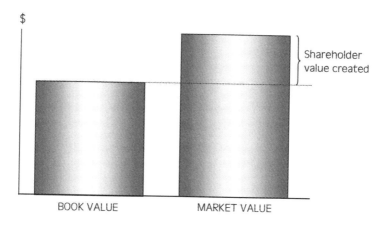

SHAREHOLDER VALUE IS CREATED WHEN MARKET VALUE EXCEEDS BOOK VALUE

The market price per share is simply the share price quoted in the financial press or, in a privately owned company, the estimated share price. The book value per share is the value of shareholders' funds as quoted in the balance sheet divided by the number of shares in issue. This tells us the value of shareholders' funds physically tied up in the business that is attributable to each share in issue.

Now let's move on to the calculation itself. Suppose we are looking at a company called Albatross Industries. Its current share data can be summarized as follows:

Number of shares in issue	20 million
Shareholders' funds (as stated in the balance sheet)	$100 million
Share price (as stated in the financial press)	$7.50

To calculate the market to book ratio we need two figures:

* **Market price per share**
  We know that this is $7.50.
* **Book value per share**
  This is the shareholders' funds of $100 million divided by the 20 million shares in issue, giving a value of $5.00 per share.

We can now calculate the market to book ratio:

$$\text{Market to book ratio } = \frac{\text{Market price per share of \$7.50}}{\text{Book value per share of \$5.00}} = 1.5$$

The market price of a share in Albatross Industries is one and a half times greater than its book value. In other words, for every $1 that has been physically invested in the business, an additional $0.50 of value has been created. This is a powerful measure but, to fully understand what it is telling us, we first need to know a little more about how share prices are set.

 The bare bones
The ability of a company to create shareholder value can be ascertained using the market to book ratio.

We noted in the previous chapter that the market price of shares is driven by expectations of future profit performance. What we have not established yet is how the exact share price is determined. For example, in the case of Albatross Industries, why is its share price set at $7.50? To understand this is to understand how shareholder value is created. What follows is a simple model of how share prices are determined. In reality the process is somewhat more involved, but the basic concept holds true.

Before going any further, we need to establish why anyone would want to buy shares in the first place. Logically people want to earn a return on their investment. The motivating factor is to obtain a higher rate of return than on alternative types of safer investment. If investors can earn 5% per annum on a savings account with a bank, they might want a rate of return of (say) 10% from shares to compensate for the additional risk. This will ultimately determine the market to book ratio of a company.

Given that share prices are driven by expectations of future profit performance, let's assume that anticipated profit for Albatross Industries is $5 million during the next year. We will now examine how this determines the market to book ratio. The five stages involved are detailed below. Study each stage carefully, as this is critical to understanding how shareholder value is created.

STAGE	KEY FIGURE	EXPLANATION
1	A **profit forecast**	The market price of shares is driven by profit expectations. In this instance, forecast profit is **$5 million** over the next year
2	is required to provide an expected **return on shareholders' funds**	Given that shareholders have $100 million invested in the business (as stated in the balance sheet), a profit of $5 million represents a **5%** rate of return on those funds
3	which provides an expected **earnings per share**	If profit is expected to be $5 million and there are 20 million shares in issue, earnings per share will be **$0.25**
4	which will determine the **share price**	Now comes the logic – read the next few lines slowly! If investors want a return of 10% and expected EPS is $0.25, the highest price they will be prepared to pay for a share is **$2.50**. At this price an EPS of $0.25 provides a 10% return. Paying more than $2.50 for a share would result in a return of less than 10%
5	which will determine the **market to book ratio**	Dividing the market price per share of $2.50 by the book value per share of $5.00 (worked out earlier in this chapter), the market to book ratio will be **0.5**

This five-stage process is summarized in the table overleaf, along with two other scenarios showing what would happen to the market to book ratio if forecast profit for the company over the next year was $10 million and what would happen if it was $20 million.

FORECASTED PROFIT	RETURN ON SHAREHOLDERS' FUNDS OF $100m	EPS (20m SHARES IN ISSUE)	MARKET PRICE OF SHARE	MARKET TO BOOK RATIO
$5 million	5%	$0.25	$2.50	0.5
$10 million	10%	$0.50	$5.00	1.0
$20 million	20%	$1.00	$10.00	2.0

THE IMPACT OF PROFIT FORECASTS ON SHARE PRICES

If forecast profit over the next year is $10 million, this would represent a 10% return on the $100 million physically invested in the company, providing an earnings per share of $0.50 (since there are 20 million shares in issue). Given that shareholders want a minimum return of 10% on their investment, the maximum they will be prepared to pay for such a share is $5.00. Comparing this against the book value per share of $5.00 produces a market to book ratio of 1.0.

If forecast profit over the next year is $20 million, this would represent a 20% return on the $100 million physically invested in the company and earnings per share would be $1.00 (given 20 million shares in issue). Investors would now be willing to pay up to $10 per share to ensure that they still achieve a rate of return of 10%. This results in a market to book ratio of 2.0 (market price per share of $10.00 divided by the book value per share of $5.00).

These three scenarios provide an insight into the market to book ratio and what it tells us about how a business is being managed. When the market to book ratio is 1, it can be seen that the rate of return being earned on shareholders' funds physically invested in the company is 10%. This is exactly the same as the rate of return that shareholders are currently looking for. When the market to book ratio is 0.5, the rate of return being achieved on shareholders' funds is only 5%, which is half the 10% return investors are looking for. When the market to book ratio is 2.0, the rate of return being achieved on shareholders' funds is 20%, which is double the 10% return investors are looking for. It follows that the market to book ratio provides an indication of how effective shareholders believe a company will be at using their funds to generate a satisfactory rate of return in the future.

Let's summarize how to interpret this ratio:

* **Less than 1**

   Shareholders' funds are being invested inefficiently. The anticipated future rate of return on funds invested is less than the rate shareholders would normally expect. Managers are destroying shareholder value.

* **1**

   The anticipated future rate of return on funds invested is the same as the rate shareholders would normally expect.

* **Greater than 1**

   Shareholders' funds are being invested efficiently. The anticipated future rate of return on funds invested is greater than the rate shareholders would normally expect. Managers are creating shareholder value.

This raises an issue. In the case of Albatross Industries, when the market to book ratio is 0.5, it would be claimed that shareholder value is being destroyed, even though the company is still expected to make a profit of $5 million. How can we argue that the company is destroying value when it is making a profit? What shareholders are looking for is an adequate rate of return. A market to book ratio that is less than 1 tells us that, even if the company is profitable, it is not expected to generate enough profit to justify the level of funds invested in it. The shareholders would be better off investing their funds elsewhere. To create value, companies need to generate enough profit to provide what is deemed a reasonable rate of return on the funds invested.

 The bare bones

Shareholder value is created when companies are expected to generate a rate of return that is higher than would normally be expected.

How efficiently are   being used by the   to increase the
shareholders' funds   management team   share price?

THE MARKET TO BOOK RATIO ANSWERS A QUESTION

Why is shareholder value important?

A strong market to book ratio is an indicator to shareholders that their funds are going to be used efficiently in the future. This provides two benefits:

* It encourages existing investors to stay with the company
* It attracts new investors

By creating demand for the shares, this should result in a healthy share price.

Failure to maintain a strong market to book ratio makes a company vulnerable. Existing shareholders may become keen to dispose of their shares. This will lead to the share price falling and increases the likelihood of the business being bought out by a predator. Why would anyone want to buy an ailing business? There are usually two motives:

* Business turnaround
* Asset stripping

One reason for buying a business that is struggling is because the new owners believe that the business can be rescued. This is typically based on the view that the way the business is currently being managed can be improved. Consequently, a change of senior management is common in this circumstance. This may well be followed by changes to the goods and services the company offers, coupled with significant changes in how the business is run. Buyouts of struggling companies usually mean significant changes ahead. The old business model is not seen to be working, so it needs to be replaced by a new one.

Another reason for buying a business that is struggling is 'asset stripping.' This means acquiring a business simply to dispose of its assets. The threat of this happening becomes particularly acute when the market to book ratio falls below 1. In this situation, the value of the net assets stated on the balance sheet exceeds the value of the company on the open market. Consequently, if someone bought the company they might be able to make a profit by simply closing it down, selling off all the assets, and paying off all the associated liabilities. This will only work where the market values of the assets are close to (or even exceed) the values quoted in the balance sheet. It follows that a market to book ratio of less than 1 is a signal to potential asset strippers that there may be an opportunity that can be exploited. However, they would have to examine the break-up value of the business carefully before they proceed.

The bare bones

Failure to create shareholder value can lead to a company being bought out, which could lead to significant management restructuring and/or asset stripping.

How can you measure the amount of shareholder value being created?

The market to book ratio is a prospective measure. It is based on how investors believe the company is going to perform in the future. As confidence in the future increases, so too will the market to book ratio. If confidence wanes, this will be reflected in a falling market to book ratio. However, shareholders will also be interested in how much shareholder value is currently being created. To address this, a concept called 'value added' has been devised. It works on a very similar principle to the market to book ratio and, like that measure, is probably best explained by means of an example.

When looking at Albatross Industries above, we noted that the company has shareholders' funds of $100 million, as reported in its balance sheet. We also assumed that shareholders are looking for a 10% annual rate of return. In order to satisfy these expectations, the company needs to deliver an annual profit of at least $10 million (which is 10% of the $100 million invested). However, if all companies are providing a similar return, why would anyone choose to buy shares specifically in Albatross Industries? To attract investors, a company needs to be seen to be generating a higher rate of return than its peers. This is where value added comes in.

Suppose that Albatross Industries produces an annual profit of $30 million, which is $20 million more than the $10 million it needed to satisfy shareholders' expectations. This additional $20 million is called value added.

Let's summarize how to calculate value added using the results of Albatross Industries:

Required profit
= Shareholders' funds x Shareholders' required rate of return
= $100 million x 10%
= $10 million
Actual profit
= $30 million
Value added
= Actual profit – Required profit
= $20 million

The company has provided shareholders with $20 million profit in excess of what they would normally expect. This provides a strong incentive to invest in Albatross Industries. The more value that is being added, the more incentive there is for shareholders to invest.

The bare bones
Value added measures the additional profit that a company generates above what shareholders would normally expect.

Stripping it down to basics...

At its most basic level, creating shareholder value can be viewed as increasing the value of the shareholders' investment. Whether or not this is being achieved can be ascertained using the market to book ratio. According to this measure, shareholder value is created when companies are expected to generate a rate of return that is higher than would be expected from similar-risk investments elsewhere. Failure to create shareholder value can lead to a company being bought out, which could, in turn, result in significant management restructuring and even asset stripping.

When it comes to identifying the amount of shareholder value that is created during a year, value added is a commonly used measure that identifies the additional profit a company generates in excess of what shareholders would normally expect.

Part Three

PROVIDING FINANCIAL CONTROL

To manage the finances of a business

you need to control where you are going

10 HOW DO YOU
CREATE A FINANCIAL PLAN?

It's that time again! You have to submit a plan for your division for the next trading year. Nobody has ever explained to you how to create a business plan – it seems to be assumed throughout the company that everybody already knows how this is done.

Perhaps you should start by planning costs. You already know what you are spending, so this should be straightforward. Unfortunately, as soon as you start to examine costs you hit a problem. How can you plan costs without knowing what sales are going to be? This seems to suggest you should start by planning sales. The problem with sales is that performance will depend on a whole range of issues including product pricing, stock availability, staffing levels, the state of the economy, competitor activity, and so on. If you are going to provide a decent sales plan, you need to show that you have taken account of all these factors. This could take weeks!

If you cannot start by planning costs because they are contingent on sales and you cannot start by planning sales because it is too complex, perhaps you should start by planning profit. This poses yet another problem. The amount of profit you will generate is dependent on sales and costs, which you have already established you do not know. Then there is the issue of cash flow – you know it is important, but how do you plan it? You are rapidly coming to the conclusion that this entire planning exercise is a complete waste of time because, even if you are able to commit some figures to paper, they will inevitably turn out to be wrong. So why bother?

Let's establish a key concept at the outset. If you want to run a profitable business, you have to start with a plan. There is an adage in the world of finance called the 'five Ps':

Poor Planning Produces Poor Performance

This is one of those sayings that all too frequently translates itself into reality, so time spent planning is always time well invested. **In this chapter we are going to look at how to bring together all the financial aspects of a business within a coherent plan that is based on sound commercial logic.**

Why have financial plans?

We have seen that shareholders invest funds in companies in order to obtain a return on their investment. It follows that in order to satisfy shareholders' expectations, businesses need to coordinate resources to ensure that they meet their targets. This is the role of financial planning. Creating financial plans, which are more commonly referred to as 'budgets,' provides a control device that can be used to ensure that the appropriate actions are being taken. If trading performance subsequently deviates from the budget, this will provide a signal to management that action may be required to ensure that commercial targets are still attained.

 The bare bones
Budgets are needed to provide a control device that can be used to ensure the attainment of commercial goals.

Do not confuse planning with forecasting – they are not the same thing. A plan details future actions that need to be taken to achieve predefined commercial goals, the most important of which is usually a profit target. A forecast, by contrast, is an estimate of what is expected to happen in the future. The distinguishing feature is the objective.

* **Budget**
  Objective: To provide a plan for future trading that will result in the attainment of pre-defined commercial targets.
* **Forecast**
  Objective: To provide an estimate of what future trading is likely to be based on the latest available information.

PLANNING IS NEEDED TO ACHIEVE OBJECTIVES

What is the difference between a forecast and a budget?

Forecasts are needed on a regular basis to ensure that resources are available to satisfy anticipated trading requirements. For example, a very important reason for needing forecasts is to plan cash flow (which as we have seen is vital to business survival).

Let's be sure that we understand the difference between resource management (which is the role of a forecast) and management control (which is the role of a budget). Suppose two friends (Adam and Louise) are planning to meet at 7.30 pm for dinner. Adam makes several telephone calls to Louise during the evening, as follows:

CALL 1 'I'm just ringing to confirm I'll see you at the Abbey restaurant at 7.30 prompt.'

CALL 2 'I've arrived home late from work. Can we please reschedule the table booking to 8 pm?'

CALL 3 'I need to stop off at a garage, I'm low on fuel. Can we change the table booking to 8.30?'

CALL 4 'I'm stuck in horrendous traffic. I won't be with you until 9.30. Since last orders at the Abbey restaurant are 9 pm, let's meet at Pierre's Brasserie: they don't close until midnight.'

Adam finally meets up with Louise at 9.30 pm. Note that his latest forecast was indeed 9.30, whereas the planned (budgeted) meeting time had been 7.30. Both pieces of information are important, but for different reasons.

✳ **Forecast**

The latest forecasted meeting time was 9.30 pm and this is the time Adam arrived. Louise needs to know this, so that she can ensure that the appropriate restaurant is booked and that she is there when Adam arrives.

✳ **Budget**

The plan was to meet at the Abbey restaurant at 7.30 pm. This was the original intention, but the actual evening did not turn out as planned. Adam should ask the question, 'Why was I two hours late?' Unless he does this, thereby learning from experience, he may well continue to be late when meeting friends, probably ending up with a life of solitude and occasional thoughts of how things might have been. If only he had understood the difference between a budget and a forecast!

Only by comparing actual performance against budget can management identify the reasons for business performance deviating from expectations. This is a prerequisite for making appropriate management decisions. It is this latter skill set that is the main focus of this chapter.

 The bare bones

Forecasts are needed to manage resources, they do not ensure that commercial goals are attained.

Can a budget ever be right?

Although budgets permeate almost every aspect of a business, they tend to be much misunderstood. Let's get some misconceptions out of the way.

Misconception 1: A budget is a weapon

Many managers equate the word 'budget' with the word 'weapon.' They claim that budgets are useful for beating people over the head with (metaphorically, of course) and telling them what they have failed to do. They also claim that budgets are useful for saying 'no' to people: 'No, you can't do that – it's not in the budget.' In fact, budgets exist to make life easier, not more difficult. Their primary function is to help managers make decisions that will ensure commercial goals are attained. Indeed, if you do not use a budget to help you make decisions, you are not using a budget at all.

Misconception 2: A budget is a numerical exercise

When managers are asked to provide a budget, they usually end up producing a schedule of figures. It is important to realize that the figures provide a summary of the budget, but they are not the budget itself. Consider the following conversation between a training manager and a finance manager at the end of a trading year.

> FINANCE MANAGER: How did the training department do last year?
> TRAINING MANAGER: Great! We had a budget of $500,000 and we spent exactly $500,000. Didn't we do well?
> FINANCE MANAGER: So how many courses did you run?
> TRAINING MANAGER: None.
> FINANCE MANAGER: Oh! So, what alternative forms of training did you initiate?
> TRAINING MANAGER: None.
> FINANCE MANAGER: So, what did you do with the $500,000?
> TRAINING MANAGER: It was wonderful! We paid for the entire department to fly to the Caribbean for a two-week all-expenses-paid vacation!

The plan (the budget) was to provide training for staff in the company, with the intention of enhancing trading performance. It was not to sponsor a two-week Caribbean holiday! Consequently, when looking at a budget it is not the figures that are the most important issue. What needs to be determined is whether or not managers are doing what they are supposed to do. A budget is a plan of action, it is not a set of numbers. Numbers may be used to summarize a plan, but they are not the plan itself.

Misconception 3: The budget is wrong

Managers often claim a budget is wrong. They then proceed to replace the budget with a forecast. Forecasts can also be wrong. If this should turn out to be the case, the forecast may need to be replaced by a 'revised forecast.' Regrettably, revised forecasts can also be wrong. This may lead to the replacement of the revised forecast with an 'updated revised forecast.' Updated revised forecasts can be wrong, so this may need to be replaced by an 'enhanced updated revised forecast.' Bad news! Enhanced updated revised forecasts can be wrong as well, so this may ultimately need to be replaced with a 'strategically realigned enhanced updated revised forecast.' Although you may have witnessed such a process in real life where a significant portion of management time is taken up continually updating and amending forecasts, this has nothing to do with the world of budgeting.

Believe it or not, a budget is only of use when someone says it is wrong. This might seem bizarre, but it is true. Suppose you are looking at last month's trading results and are informed that trading is exactly as expected. This means that the actual figures will be identical to the budgeted figures. What is the point of looking at two sets of identical numbers? Surely it is when the actual and budgeted results differ that the budget comes into its own. It is saying something has happened that we did not expect, so what are we going to do about it? This is definitely not the time to take the view: 'The budget is wrong, so let's ignore it.'

Creating a plan for a business is much the same as planning a holiday. You decide you want to go to the coast for a few days. Filled with enthusiasm, you sit down with a map and plan your route. Before you know it, you are in the car and on your way when you hear on the radio there has been an accident on the road ahead and a lengthy queue has already formed. To avoid this, you turn off at the next exit. A course of action you certainly should not take at this point is to declare the map is wrong and throw it out the window! What you need to do is sit down and study the map. You look at where you are now (which may appear to be in the middle of nowhere) and where you planned to be. On the basis of this comparison, you may be able to identify another route that will get you to your destination by the evening. Alternatively, you may decide it is now impractical to get to your destination today, so you will have to stop off somewhere along the route. Neither of these decisions can be made unless you take time to compare your actual location with your planned (budgeted) location, even if they are miles apart. The same principle applies in business.

Let's summarize what we have learned from these misconceptions.

THE MISCONCEPTION	THE FACTS
'A budget is a weapon'	Budgets are there to help you make decisions
'A budget is a numerical exercise'	Budgets are plans of action
'The budget is wrong'	Budgets enable you to respond to changing circumstances

Ultimately, budgets are there to help control the business, by providing a plan against which actual performance can be continually compared, with any deviations being used to indicate where management action is required. Of course, none of this can be achieved unless a budget is created in the first place.

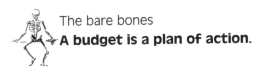 The bare bones
A budget is a plan of action.

How do you create a budget?

Before examining the planning process, we need to establish what period of time the plan covers. In this respect, it is common to encounter three types of budget.

* **Short-term budget**
This is sometimes referred to as an 'operational budget,' typically

covering one year, containing detailed plans relating to each operation undertaken within the business.

∗ **Medium-term budget**

This is sometimes referred to as a 'tactical budget,' typically covering between two and five years, containing detailed plans for the company but at a corporate level only.

∗ **Long-term budget**

This is sometimes referred to as a 'strategic budget,' typically covering five years or more, containing summary plans regarding how the company wishes to develop in the long term.

Regardless of the type of budget being prepared, the principles of how it should be prepared remain the same. Suppose you are about to set the budget for your entire company for the forthcoming year. Where would you start? There are so many issues to consider: the state of the economy, anticipated sales, proposed marketing activity, competitor activity, the product offer, pricing strategy, inventory levels, supplier terms, staffing levels, equipment needs, and so on. This would seem to suggest that financial planning is a very involved process. Fortunately, the principles of setting a budget are straightforward, even if their practical application may be a bit more involved.

It does not matter whether you are setting a budget for a multinational corporation, a small family business, or an individual department – the first step is always the same. You need to ask one question:

∗ **What is limiting our business?**

The answer to this question is known as the 'principal budget factor' or 'limiting factor.' The reason it enjoys such a grandiose title is that it should drive the entire budgetary process. This is the factor that is currently restricting business activity.

It is at this stage that the significance of the various types of budget mentioned above will become apparent. Suppose a manufacturing company, when creating its annual budget, has identified production capacity as its limiting factor: there is a limit to how much it can produce. This will constrain its sales, which in turn will constrain its potential profit. If the company was creating a medium-term or long-term budget this may not be the limiting factor, since the company may envisage building another factory within the next five years, thereby removing this constraint. The limiting factor in a longer-term budget might be completely different, possibly market share. This would result in the business being constrained by the size of the potential market and the proportion of that market it is able to capture. So, although the initial question is always the same, the potential answers may vary considerably.

 The bare bones
The first step when creating a budget is to ask a question: 'What is limiting our business?'

Let's look at how this approach applies when preparing an operational budget at a corporate level, since operational budgets (covering one year) tend to be the most common type encountered in practice. Suppose we are looking at a manufacturing company and ask the question: 'What is limiting our business?' It might be the potential market – there is a practical limit to the number of customers the business will attract. It might be capacity – there is a limit to the number of products that can physically be produced. It might be finance – there is a limit to the cash available within the business. It might be staffing – there is a limit to the number of appropriately trained employees who can be recruited. The list could go on. This presents us with a problem. If all these issues are deemed to be relevant, which is the principal budget factor? In this circumstance the principal budget factor is the issue that we believe will constrain the business first.

Having identified the principal budget factor, we can develop a sales expectation. This is achieved by asking a question:

✳ **What sales can be anticipated given the limiting factor?**

The exact wording of this question may need to be adjusted depending on the limiting factor that has been identified. In the case of our manufacturing company, this question might take one of several forms:

* What sales can be anticipated given our limited customer base?
* What sales can be anticipated given our limited production capacity?
* What sales can be anticipated given our limited cash resources?
* What sales can be anticipated given our limited availability of suitably trained employees?

and so on.

Once the sales plan has been created, only then can the expense plans be addressed. For each type of expense, a question needs to be asked:

* What costs can be anticipated given planned sales?

This leads us on to the next question:

* What profit can be anticipated given planned sales and costs?

Having established the link between sales and profit, we can then go on to address the relationship between sales and assets by asking:

* What current assets are required to support planned sales?
* What fixed assets are required to support planned sales?

Having identified the assets required, we can move on to the final question:

* What level of funds will be required to finance the planned assets?

What we have identified here is a structured approach to creating a budget. Although the exact approach adopted may vary from company to company, the core principles will remain unchanged.

STAGE 1
What is limiting our business?

STAGE 2
What **sales** can be anticipated given the limiting factor?

STAGE 3
What **costs** can be anticipated given planned sales?

STAGE 4
What **profit** can be anticipated given planned sales and costs?

STAGE 5
What **current assets** are required to support planned sales?

STAGE 6
What **fixed assets** are required to support planned sales?

STAGE 7
What level of **funds** will be required to finance the planned assets?

A STRUCTURED APPROACH TO CREATING A BUDGET

The budget process can be seen to comprise six elements:

* **Sales**   * **Current assets**
* **Costs**   * **Fixed assets**
* **Profit**   * **Funds**

In Chapter 3 ('How do you make profit?') we saw how making profit is a process. This is reproduced opposite showing where the six elements of the budget process fit in.

What we are describing here is a commercial plan. Each stage builds on the previous stage. This is very different to another approach that is sometimes encountered in practice: the 'add on 10%' principle,

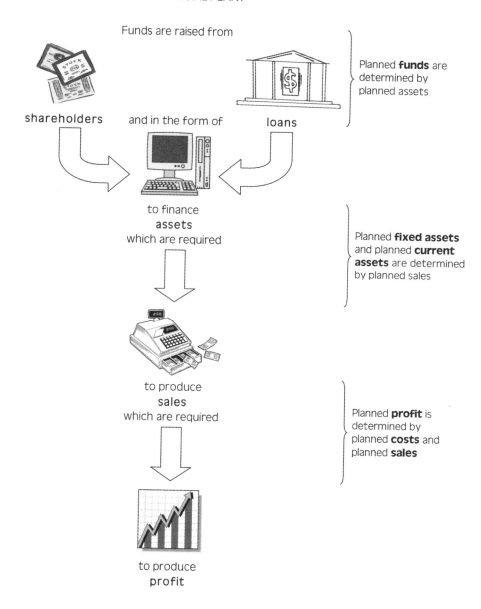

Funds are raised from

shareholders · and in the form of · loans

Planned **funds** are determined by planned assets

to finance
assets
which are required

Planned **fixed assets** and planned **current assets** are determined by planned sales

to produce
sales
which are required

Planned **profit** is determined by planned **costs** and planned **sales**

to produce
profit

THE PROFIT-MAKING PROCESS

where managers simply add a few percentage points on to the previous period's figures. This is nothing more than a numerical exercise – it is definitely not a budget!

Commercial planner   Non-commercial planner

How do you agree on a budget?

Some managers regard budgeting as a crystal ball exercise. When creating a budget, they believe all that needs to be done is to provide an estimate of what is going to happen in the future. Having formulated their best estimates, these become the budget.

If only real life were that simple. Sometimes, particularly with very small businesses, that is the budget process. Best estimates of future trading are committed to paper, possibly by a single owner or by a small group of managers. If it is felt the figures are achievable, these estimates become the budget. However, particularly in larger organizations, the budget setting process can be rather more involved. Although variations are common in practice, a basic model that is pursued by many organizations (in some shape or form) is described below.

The first point to note is that quite often two budgetary processes are taking place in tandem. At a company level the board of directors will prepare a 'corporate budget.' At the same time, managers will be preparing plans for their own respective sections of the business. These plans are known as 'functional budgets' as they represent a plan for a specific function (such as production, distribution, marketing, or human resources). Whether plans are being created at a corporate level, at a division level, or even at a department level, the approach adopted should be the same as that detailed earlier in this chapter. Start by asking the question: 'What is limiting our business?' This will facilitate the creation of a sales plan from which all other plans will follow. When both the corporate budget and the functional budgets have been completed, they need to be reconciled. Ultimately, the functional budgets should aggregate up to the corporate budget. Regrettably this rarely occurs in practice, so a review process is required.

The review process involves aggregating the functional budgets and comparing the total figures with those contained in the corporate budget. Inevitably differences will be identified, resulting in the need to make adjustments to the functional budgets and/or the corporate budget.

Corporate budget

Review process
reconciles the corporate budget to the functional budgets

Functional budgets

AGREEING THE BUDGET – THE REVIEW PROCESS

The objective of the review process is to ensure that when all the functional budgets are aggregated, they reconcile to the corporate budget. To achieve this, three alternative approaches tend to be encountered in practice.

✳ **Bottom up**

Functional budgets are aggregated and form the basis for a revised corporate budget. The corporate budget is amended while the functional budgets remain unaltered.

✱ *Advantage*: Based on budgets that are deemed to be achievable by the management team.

✱ *Disadvantage*: May not produce the return desired by shareholders.

✳ **Top down**

The corporate budget forms the basis for revised functional budgets. The functional budgets are adjusted while the corporate budget remains unchanged.

✱ *Advantage*: Based on a budget that aims to provide a satisfactory return to shareholders (as identified by the board of directors).

✱ *Disadvantage*: The functional budgets may not be viewed as achievable by managers.

✳ **Bottom up + Top down**

Functional budgets and the corporate budget are all adjusted to provide plans that are deemed attainable at all levels within the business.

✱ *Advantage*: Provides a budget that should deliver an adequate return to shareholders, while also being regarded as achievable by managers.

✱ *Disadvantage*: More complex to implement than the previous two approaches.

The most common approach encountered in practice is the last one, which is a hybrid of the top-down and bottom-up approaches. In the light of the functional budgets, the corporate budget is reviewed and amended according to what is deemed achievable. Managers are then invited to resubmit their functional budgets, but with more specific commercial guidelines being provided. At the end of this process, the aggregated functional budgets should correspond far more closely to the amended corporate budget and only minor adjustments should then be required to ensure that they reconcile completely.

Stripping it down to basics...

Budgets are needed in every business to provide a control device that ensures commercial targets are achieved. Forecasts are different: their role is to allocate resources to meet anticipated trading requirements.

The first stage in creating a budget is to ask a question: 'What is limiting our business?' The answer to this question is known as the principal budget factor (or limiting factor) and this forms the basis on which a sales plan can be created, which in turn forms the basis for all other cost and asset plans. Once these have been created, the last stage of the planning process demands the reconciliation of the corporate budget (produced by the board of directors) to the various functional budgets (produced by the individual managers) by means of a review process. The review process tends to adopt one of three forms: bottom up, top down, or a hybrid of these two approaches.

11 HOW DO YOU MANAGE COSTS?

'We must focus all our attention on sales. A dramatic improvement in sales performance is needed if we are to make a profit this year. From now on I want you to think about sales every working minute of every working day!' The chief executive picks up her papers and leaves the assembled managers to reflect on her words. Why didn't someone say something? It just doesn't make any sense. Your company already has an annual turnover in excess of $100 million and yet the chief executive is saying sales are too low. Just what level of sales do you need to make profit? How is it that companies exist that have sales of just a few thousand dollars and make a profit, while you are being told that sales of $100 million are not enough?

To understand why some companies need high sales to make a profit while other companies can be profitable with far lower sales demands an understanding of costs. **In this chapter we are going to look at the management of costs and how this can affect the relationship between sales and profit.**

What drives costs?

Regrettably, the relationship between sales and profit is not an obvious one. Sales can go up while profit goes down. Sales can go down while profit goes up. What is causing this potentially perverse relationship is what is going on in between – costs.

To run a profitable business, you need to understand the principles of cost management. If you cannot control costs, no matter how high your sales may be profit will not be forthcoming. So how do you control costs? All systems of cost control rely on one word: expectations. You must have expectations of what costs are going to be if you want to control them. If costs differ from these expectations, you need to identify why these differences have arisen and thereby determine whether or not any corrective action is required.

At a personal level you exercise cost expectations all the time. You have expectations of what various goods and services should cost and on this basis you are able to make a buy or reject decision. If you were given the opportunity to purchase a brand-new, top-of-the-range sports car for $5,000, would you accept? In all likelihood you would, because even though you may not know the list price of the vehicle, you have an expectation that the true value is far higher than $5,000. By contrast, suppose you were offered a deluxe A4 laminating kit, again brand new, for $200. Unless you happen to be heavily into laminating (maybe you subscribe to *Laminators Weekly* and already own a copy of the classic text *Laminating for Fun*), it is unlikely you know what such a device should cost you. As a result, you will be unable to decide whether or not you are being offered a bargain (assuming you want a laminating kit in the first place!). The same principle applies in business. How can you possibly decide if you are spending too much or too little, if you do not know what the cost ought to be in the first place?

 The bare bones
In order to control costs, you must have expectations of what costs are going to be.

In order to develop expectations of what costs ought to be, we need to understand what drives them. Costs can be divided into two broad categories according to how they behave.

✳ **Fixed cost**

A fixed cost is a cost that is not directly affected by sales. Regardless of whether sales go up or down, there is no reason this cost should alter. A typical example of a fixed cost in many businesses would be rent. Rent has to be paid for premises no matter what the level of sales is. However, the rent payable on a property can change. This means, ironically, that fixed costs can vary. The point to note is they do not vary with sales.

✳ **Variable cost**
A variable cost is a cost that is driven by sales. If sales go up 10%, this cost should go up 10%. If sales go down 10%, this cost should go down 10%. A good example of a variable cost in many businesses would be the cost of goods sold. If sales double, it is logical to conclude that the amount of inventory sold will have doubled. Conversely if sales halve, it usually follows that the amount of inventory sold has halved.

When trying to apply this cost distinction in practice, it is not uncommon to encounter a cost that is not totally fixed but is not totally variable either. In such a situation the following approach tends to be adopted:

✳ **If the cost is primarily sales driven, it is treated as a variable cost**
✳ **If the cost is primarily independent of sales, it is treated as a fixed cost**

By dividing costs into these two categories, we are able to develop expectations of how costs will behave in the future.

✳ **Sales increase**
Variable costs should increase by the same proportion. For example, if sales increase by 10%, variable costs should increase by 10%. Fixed costs should remain unaltered.

✳ **Sales decrease**
Variable costs should decrease by the same proportion. For example, if sales decrease by 10%, variable costs should decrease by 10%. Fixed costs should remain unaltered.

The bare bones
In order to build expectations of future behavior, costs in business are commonly divided into two categories:
* **Fixed costs**
* **Variable costs**

How do costs affect the
relationship between sales and profit?

Having established the difference between fixed costs and variable costs, we are now in a position to make sense of the relationship between sales and profit. Probably the easiest way to understand this relationship is to examine it graphically.

Let's build up the logic starting with the relationship between sales and fixed costs. When sales increase, fixed costs remain unaltered. We can look at how this would be presented on a graph.

THE RELATIONSHIP BETWEEN SALES AND FIXED COSTS

As sales increase, fixed costs remain unaltered, resulting in a horizontal fixed costs line.

Now let's look at the relationship between sales and variable costs.

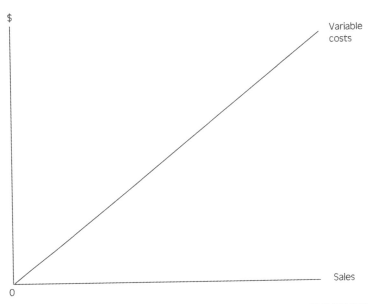

THE RELATIONSHIP BETWEEN SALES AND VARIABLE COSTS

When sales are zero, there are no variable costs. As sales increase, so too will variable costs. This results in an upward-sloping variable costs line emanating from the origin.

Given that most businesses have fixed and variable costs, by combining the two previous graphs we can see what happens to total costs in a company as sales increase.

The top graph opposite may need a little more explanation. When sales are zero, fixed costs still have to be paid but there are no variable costs. As sales increase, although fixed costs remain unaltered, variable costs increase. This results in a total cost line sloping upwards from the left (where sales are nil and only fixed costs are incurred) to the right (where sales are increasing and both fixed costs and variable costs are being incurred).

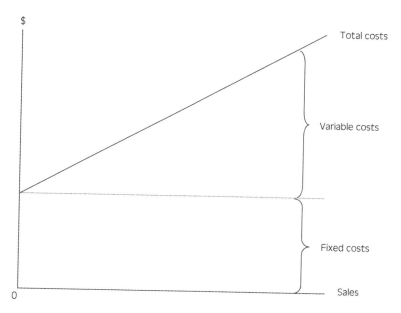

THE RELATIONSHIP BETWEEN SALES AND TOTAL COSTS

Now let's look a little more closely at sales. The role of sales is to generate revenue.

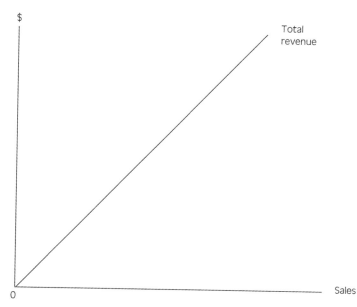

THE RELATIONSHIP BETWEEN SALES AND TOTAL REVENUE

When sales are zero, total revenue will be zero. As sales increase, total revenue will increase. This results in an upward-sloping line emanating from the origin.

Having identified the total cost line and the total revenue line, we can combine the two to show the relationship between sales and profit.

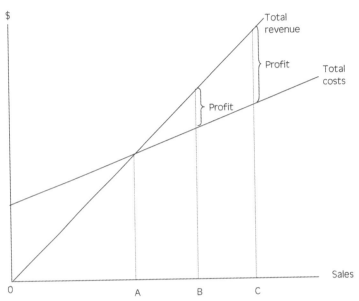

THE RELATIONSHIP BETWEEN TOTAL REVENUE AND TOTAL COSTS

This is where the fun really begins! Although it may look confusing at the outset, this graph is really quite straightforward. Just allow for the fact it may take a few minutes for the logic to sink in. There are three points on this latest graph that warrant particular attention.

A   At this level of sales, total revenue equals total costs: the company will break even. If sales are to the left of this position, total costs exceed total revenue, resulting in a loss. If sales are to the right of this position, total revenue exceeds total costs, resulting in a profit.

B   At this level of sales, total revenue exceeds total costs, so a profit is being generated. The actual level of profit being produced is the gap between total revenue and total costs, as indicated by the bracket. The larger this gap is, the more profit is being achieved.

C At this level of sales, the gap between total revenue and total costs is approximately double the size of the gap at point B. In other words, profit being achieved at point C is double the profit being achieved at point B. To achieve this profit increase, the sales increase from point B to point C is only approximately 30%. This indicates that if sales increase by 30% from point B to point C, profit will double. Examining the reverse situation, if sales drop from point C to point B, this results in a halving of profit.

By examining these points on the graph, we are able to identify two very important features that are pertinent to most types of business:

* **A minimum level of sales is required to break even**
  A certain level of sales needs to be attained just to cover costs.
* **Profit is very sensitive to changes in sales**
  When the break-even point is exceeded, a 10% increase in sales will result in a more than 10% increase in profit, while a 10% decrease in sales will result in a more than 10% decrease in profit.

The reason for these two phenomena is the existence of fixed costs. If a business only has variable costs, the relationship between sales and profit is far more straightforward: no sales equals no profit, lots of sales equals lots of profit, halving the sales halves the profit, while doubling the sales doubles the profit.

Is there an optimal cost structure for a business?

Is it better to be a primarily fixed cost or a primarily variable cost business? Striking the balance between fixed and variable costs determines the relationship between sales and profit. To fully appreciate the impact of these two cost types, let's examine two extreme cases: a totally fixed cost business and a totally variable cost business.

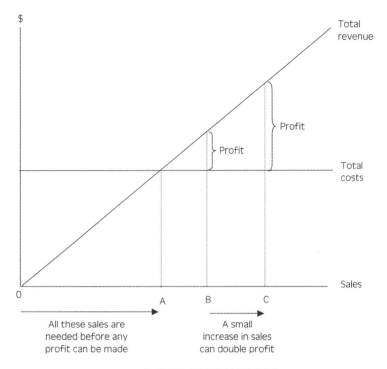

A FIXED COST BUSINESS

In the fixed cost business, sales have to reach point A before a profit is made. By contrast, in the variable cost business, profit will be made from the very first sale. Consequently a primarily variable cost business will achieve profit far more quickly than a primarily fixed cost business. It follows that the cost structure of a business affects its risk. Any business that requires commitment to a high level of fixed costs at the outset is potentially risky, since it requires a high level of sales to break even. This is in stark contrast to a primarily variable cost business, where it is virtually impossible to make a loss (provided that the variable costs are managed effectively), since only minimal sales need to be attained before profits can be generated.

This highlights the advantage of a variable cost business:

* **In a primarily variable cost business, very few sales are needed before the business starts to generate profit**
* **In a primarily fixed cost business, a high level of sales may be needed before the business starts to generate a profit**

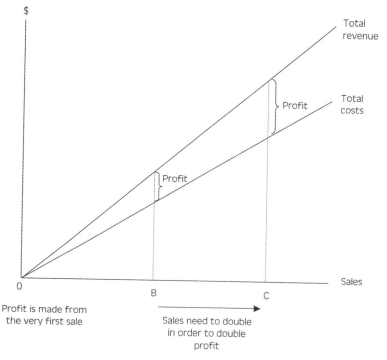

A VARIABLE COST BUSINESS

Suppose you decide to go into business selling furniture. One approach is to manufacture the furniture yourself and open a shop to sell it. This will require investment in production facilities, a showroom, and sales staff. Before you can make a profit, you need a high level of sales to cover these costs. An alternative approach is to outsource production to an established manufacturer and sell direct to the consumer via the internet. The fixed costs in this latter instance are far lower, thus demanding lower sales for the business to cover its costs.

 The bare bones

The advantage of a primarily variable cost business, compared with a primarily fixed cost business, is that it needs far fewer sales to generate profit.

Based on our findings so far, you may be wondering why anyone would even consider investing in a fixed cost business. Returning to the graphical representation of the fixed cost business, you can see that at point B the business is making a profit, where the profit achieved is the gap between the total revenue line and the total costs line. If the company wanted to double its profit (i.e. double the size of the gap), sales would need to increase to point C. By looking at the graph, it can be seen that sales have not needed to double to achieve this result. That is to say, a relatively small increase in sales will result in a 100% increase in profit.

Let's compare this with the graph for the variable cost business. Once again, at point B the company is making a profit. However, if this company wanted to double its profit, sales again would need to increase to point C but in this instance this represents a doubling of sales. To achieve a 100% increase in profit, a 100% increase in sales is required. This highlights the advantage of a fixed cost business:

* **In a primarily variable cost business, a 10% increase in sales will result in profit increasing by approximately 10%.**
* **In a primarily fixed cost business (assuming that it is already profitable), a 10% increase in sales will result in profit increasing by significantly more than 10%.**

The bare bones
The advantage of a primarily fixed cost business is that, for a given increase in sales, it can grow profit at a faster rate than a primarily variable cost business.

The table opposite summarizes the advantages and disadvantages of adopting a specific cost structure within a business. Managing the cost structure of a business enables us to manage the relationship between sales and profit.

BUSINESS TYPE	ADVANTAGE	DISADVANTAGE
Primarily variable cost	Low sales needed to achieve profit	High rate of growth in sales needed to achieve high rate of growth in profit
Primarily fixed cost	Small rate of growth in sales can result in high rate of growth in profit	High sales needed to achieve profit

Stripping it down to basics...

In order to control costs, you must have expectations of what costs are going to be. Costs in business are commonly divided into two types: fixed costs and variable costs. The cost structure of a business affects the relationship between sales and profit. The advantage of being a primarily variable cost business is that only minimal sales are required to make profit, but the disadvantage is that profit growth will be limited to the rate of growth in sales. The advantage of being a primarily fixed cost business is that a small increase in sales can lead to a dramatic increase in profit, but the disadvantage is that a high level of sales is required initially before any profit is made at all.

12 HOW DO YOU MANAGE SALES?

When it comes to sales planning, where do you start? Anticipated sales can be one of the most problematic and contentious figures you are ever asked to produce. You know it can be affected by a wide variety of factors such as the products you sell, how you price them, your methods of distribution, the sales skills of your staff, the type of marketing you undertake, and the state of the economy. In order to produce even a vaguely realistic sales figure, it would appear you need take account of all these factors. This may well be leading you to the conclusion that sales planning can be a very involved process.

The good news is that because sales planning is such a critical issue in business, methods have been developed to simplify the process. **In this chapter we are going to look at a powerful technique that enables realistic sales plans to be produced in a straightforward, time-effective manner.**

How can you ensure that sales will be profitable?

Sales are at the heart of every business. Sales determine costs, asset requirements, and ultimately the profit achieved. Regrettably, producing sales is no guarantee of profit. Successful sales management, from a financial perspective, is all about producing a robust plan at the outset that will result in a profitable business.

In the previous chapter you were introduced to fixed and variable costs and how they affect the relationship between sales and profit. Building on this cost distinction, a formula exists that not only explains the relationship between sales and profit, but also greatly simplifies the sales planning process. It is encapsulated within a technique known as 'CVP analysis.'

To understand what CVP stands for, we need to revisit the profit calculation:

Profit in a period = Sales in a period
                    LESS Costs incurred to produce that period's
                        sales

CVP stands for the three factors that appear in this equation:

* **Costs**
* **Volume of sales**
* **Profit**

In fact, CVP analysis is an abbreviation for 'cost–volume–profit analysis'. This technique explains how costs, the volume of sales, and profit interrelate and by so doing provides a powerful planning tool. It can provide in minutes plans that many people could spend days or even weeks trying to prepare.

Although the technique does involve some simple mathematics, don't let this deter you. Its benefits far outweigh any minor headaches you may have as you work through the calculations. All you should really concentrate on is the logic – if you understand the logic, the figures will make perfect sense.

The bare bones
CVP analysis enables sales plans to be developed in a matter of minutes.

How can you plan sales quickly?

One of the reasons for the justifiable popularity of CVP analysis is that it's fast. Let us build the logic step by step. Suppose you are considering setting up your own clothing store and what appears to be an ideal site has just become available to rent. You estimate you will need $750,000 at the outset to fit out the store, fill it with inventory, purchase equipment, and cover various other initial expenses. Is this an opportunity worth considering? The answer to this question depends on your ability to generate sales, and this is where CVP analysis comes to the rescue.

The most common application for CVP analysis is to help identify a planned sales figure. In order to achieve this, the technique can be viewed as comprising three distinct stages. The first stage involves establishing why you want sales in the first place. In other words, how much would you like to earn? There are only two reasons any business wants sales:

* **To pay its regular expenses**
  A business will incur certain expenses regardless of whether sales take place or not. These are its fixed costs and need to be paid.
* **To make a profit**
  Businesses need to generate a profit to provide a return to their investors.

In your clothing business you will have to pay fixed costs such as rent, heating and lighting, telephone, salaries, and so forth. In addition, you will want a return on the $750,000 you are planning to invest. Suppose you estimate that your fixed costs during the first year of trading will be $250,000. In addition, you would like to achieve a profit of $150,000 (which represents a 20% return on your initial investment of $750,000). We have now established that you would like to have enough sales to

* **Pay your annual fixed costs of $250,000**
* **Plus provide a profit of $150,000**

By adding these two figures together we can see that you need to earn $400,000 during the next year.

Now we hit a problem. As you start to generate sales, you will start to incur variable (sales-related) costs. This brings us on to the second stage of CVP analysis. In order to calculate the elusive sales figure, we need to establish how much you want to make on each sale. To achieve this, CVP analysis introduces a concept called 'contribution,' where

Contribution per sale = Revenue from the sale
LESS Variable costs incurred to produce the sale

If you sell an item of clothing, the revenue from the sale will be the selling price, while the main variable cost will be the cost of the item being sold. On this basis, if you buy a jacket for $60 and subsequently sell it for $100, you will achieve a contribution of $40. This is $40 toward your total earnings target of $400,000, which explains why contribution is so called: it is an abbreviation for 'contribution toward fixed costs and profit.' This concept is easy to grasp when we're dealing with a single-product business. However, what if you intend to sell a range of clothes that are bought and sold at a variety of prices? What would a contribution per sale mean in this situation?

It is common practice in a multiproduct business to talk about contribution per $1 sale. In other words, on every $1 that goes into the till, on average how much is profit after only paying for variable costs? We have already established that when you buy a jacket for $60 and subsequently sell it for $100, you make $40 contribution. Another way of saying the same thing is that you will make $0.40 per $1 sale. This principle can be applied to any multiproduct business. If you decide you want to sell a wide range of clothing and you want to make $0.40 per $1 sale, you may end up selling some items that make more than $0.40 and other items that make less than $0.40, but on average you intend to make $0.40 per $1 sale. Let's assume you are happy to proceed on this basis.

We now come to the third and final stage of CVP analysis: we need to establish what sales you need. By combining your required

earnings with your anticipated contribution per $1 sale, we can iden-
tify the required sales by applying the following formula:

$$\text{Required sales} = \frac{\text{Required earnings of } \$400,000}{\text{Planned contribution of } \$0.40 \text{ per } \$1 \text{ sale}}$$

$$= \$1,000,000$$

If you generate a contribution of $0.40 on every $1 sale, you will
need sales of $1 million in order to pay your fixed costs of $250,000
and leave you with a profit of $150,000.

Let's review how we arrived at this result. We followed a three-
stage process:

Stage 1 Decide how much you want to earn in total
Stage 2 Decide how much you want to earn on each sale
Stage 3 Calculate the sales required

This enabled us to identify a sales requirement of $1 million, but
it did take several paragraphs to arrive at this result. CVP analysis lets
us speed up the process by providing a formula that allows us to identify the sales required to achieve any level of profit. Let's re-examine
how we combined each of the above stages to identify the sales
required for your clothing business.

1 Decide how much you want to earn in total
This was achieved by adding together the expected fixed costs of
the business and the required profit:

Planned fixed costs of $250,000
PLUS Planned profit of $150,000
= $400,000

2 Decide how much you want to earn on each sale
This was achieved by planning a contribution per $1 sale, where

Planned contribution per $1 sale = $0.40

3 Calculate the sales required

By dividing contribution per $1 sale into required earnings, we identified the sales required to achieve the profit target:

Required earnings of $400,000
divided by
Planned contribution of $0.40 per $1 sale
= $1,000,000

A faster way of arriving at the same result is to combine all three stages into a single formula:

$$\text{Required sales} = \frac{\text{Planned fixed costs} + \text{Planned profit}}{\text{Planned contribution per \$1 sale}}$$

This is the CVP formula. Applying this to your clothing business, we are able to identify the required sales far more quickly than previously:

$$\begin{aligned} \text{Required sales} &= \frac{\text{Planned fixed costs} + \text{Planned profit}}{\text{Planned contribution per \$1 sale}} \\[2mm] &= \frac{\$250,000 + \$150,000}{\$0.40} \\[2mm] &= \$1,000,000 \end{aligned}$$

This highlights a powerful attribute of CVP analysis: it is fast. To identify the sales required to achieve a profit target, only three figures are required: planned fixed costs, planned profit, and planned contribution per $1 sale. When these have been identified, we can calculate the required sales figure in a matter of seconds. This helps explain the popularity of this technique.

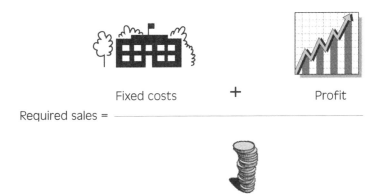

$$\text{Required sales} = \frac{\text{Fixed costs} \quad + \quad \text{Profit}}{\text{Contribution per \$1 sale}}$$

CVP ANALYSIS COMBINES THREE FIGURES

How can you decide if a sales plan is achievable?

There is another reason CVP analysis is so popular. It removes the need for a conventional sales forecast. When you come up with a new business initiative, the first question that is normally asked is, 'What do you think sales are going to do?' Regrettably, if you want to find one figure in any business that is wrong, it will nearly always be the sales plan. For example, in some businesses the weather can have a dramatic impact on sales. Professional meteorologists can have problems accurately forecasting the weather for the next 24 hours. An accurate sales forecast would in many businesses demand the ability to forecast the weather up to one year in advance! Despite this, many businesses are happy to start the planning process with a figure that everyone agrees will be wrong: the sales plan. This is then used as the basis for planning inventory, staffing levels, property requirements, and so on. CVP challenges this approach. Instead of starting with what we don't know (i.e. what sales are going to be), why not start with what we do know?

In your clothing business, you will have a reasonable idea what clothes are going to cost you and it is down to you how much to charge your customers, so contribution per $1 sale is very much under your control. In addition, it is up to you how much you are prepared to spend running the business, so you have a large degree of control over the fixed costs. Furthermore, it is up to you how much profit you want to make in order to provide a reasonable return on funds invested. As a result, you should be able to plan all these issues with a reasonable degree of accuracy.

Based on these figures, CVP analysis will provide the figure you do not know: the sales figure. This makes sales planning far more straightforward. In the case of your clothing business, based on our previous assumptions, all you have to do is ask a question:

＊ **Do we expect sales to be at least $1 million?**

If the answer is yes, this means that the profit target of $150,000 is achievable, so the proposed strategy is viable – you have a plan. If the answer is no, you are back to the drawing board. The proposed strategy will not work, so you will need to adjust either the profit target or the fixed costs or the contribution per $1 sale. You might even want to adjust two of these factors or even all three.

Note how CVP analysis simplifies the decision-making process. Imagine you are leaving the office at the end of a busy day. If someone asked you what time you were going to arrive home to the minute, that would be a forecast and it is almost certain to be wrong. However, if someone asked if you expected to arrive home before midnight, that would be a far easier question to answer. CVP analysis works the same way. It adopts the approach that instead of trying to estimate what sales are going to be in the future, you just decide if sales are expected to be greater than or less than a specified value. To ask a manager to provide a sales forecast that is accurate to the dollar will not only result in a lot of hard work, it will also result in a number that is bound to be wrong. However, asking a manager whether or not sales are expected to be more or less than $1 million next year is a far easier question to answer.

The bare bones

CVP analysis enables strategies to be readily assessed by providing a minimum level of sales needed for a strategy to work.

We have now identified two significant benefits associated with CVP analysis:

* It is simple to apply
* It makes decision making straightforward

The good news does not stop here. There is a third benefit associated with this technique:

* It enables alternative strategies to be readily assessed

How can you evaluate alternative sales strategies?

So far, when looking at your clothing business, we have explored one strategy that could make you $150,000 profit. In reality, there are a multitude of ways this might be achieved. Sales planning is not just about finding a sales figure that you believe is achievable. It also commonly involves looking at a variety of strategies and identifying which is the most viable.

Suppose you believe that there is capacity to handle more than $1 million worth of sales in your store. This has led to you considering two further strategies that could potentially increase sales:

* You believe you could increase sales by offering more competitive selling prices. In fact, you are considering reducing contribution from $0.40 per $1 sale to $0.25 per $1 sale. That is, you are prepared to earn $0.15 less per $1 sale in order to stimulate sales.
* As an alternative to reducing selling prices, you are considering spending $50,000 on an advertising campaign.

You believe that any resulting increase in sales can be handled by existing staff and without any significant increase in other store running costs. What you want to determine is which strategy has the greater chance of success. Unfortunately, trying to estimate the additional sales that will result from reducing prices or from advertising will inevitably result in a huge element of guesswork. This is where CVP analysis comes to the fore. It takes the view that instead of trying to guess what sales are going to be, we should determine what sales have to be to ensure that the strategy will work.

In the first alternative scenario, we are considering reducing the contribution to $0.25 per $1 sale. We have already noted that we believe any increase in sales can be handled without the need to increase store running costs. As a result, fixed costs in the CVP formula will remain unchanged at $250,000. Also, the business still needs to provide a return on the $750,000 invested, which has already been set at $150,000. This is all the information we need to calculate a new sales requirement:

$$\text{Required sales} = \frac{\text{Planned fixed costs} + \text{Planned profit}}{\text{Planned contribution per \$1 sale}}$$

$$= \frac{\$250,000 + \$150,000}{\$0.25}$$

$$= \$1,600,000$$

If the contribution per $1 sale is reduced from $0.40 to $0.25 while maintaining fixed costs at their current level of $250,000, sales of $1.6 million would need to be achieved in order still to produce a profit of $150,000. Comparing this against the original scenario that required sales of $1 million, we can conclude that sales would need to increase by 60% in order to compensate for earning $0.15 less per $1 sale. This makes the decision making far more straightforward:

✳ **Do you think that by reducing selling prices so that contribution falls from $0.40 per $1 sale to $0.25 per $1 sale, sales will increase by a minimum of $600,000?**

If you believe this is achievable, the strategy could potentially result in increased profit. However, if you believe there is little chance of increasing sales by 60%, you should not proceed with reducing prices as sales will be insufficient to achieve the targeted level of profit.

In the second alternative scenario, we are considering spending $50,000 on advertising, while maintaining contribution at its original level of $0.40 per $1 sale. Given that we are talking about a $50,000 increase in running costs, this will have the effect of increasing fixed costs in the CVP formula by $50,000, from $250,000 to $300,000. As previously, the business still needs to provide a return on funds invested and the profit target has already been set at $150,000. The sales that would now be required are as follows:

$$\text{Required sales} = \frac{\text{Planned fixed costs} + \text{Planned profit}}{\text{Planned contribution per \$1 sale}}$$

$$= \frac{\$300,000 + \$150,000}{\$0.40}$$

$$= \$1,125,000$$

If fixed costs increase by $50,000 while maintaining contribution per $1 sale at its original level, sales of $1,125,000 would need to be achieved in order to produce a profit of $150,000. Once again, comparing this against the original scenario that required sales of $1 million, we can conclude that in this instance sales would need to increase by 12.5% in order to compensate for a $50,000 increase in expenditure. As previously, this makes the decision making straightforward:

✳ **Do you think that by spending $50,000 on advertising, sales will increase by a minimum of $125,000?**

If the answer is yes, the strategy could potentially result in increased profit. If the answer is no, do not spend $50,000 on advertising as sales will be insufficient to achieve the targeted level of profit.

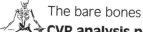
The bare bones
CVP analysis provides three distinct benefits when creating a sales plan:
   * **It is simple to apply**
   * **It makes decision making straightforward**
   * **It enables alternative scenarios to be readily assessed**

So far we have used CVP analysis to assess three different scenarios, the results of which are tabulated below.

SCENARIO	CONTRIBUTION PER $1 SALE	FIXED COSTS	PROFIT	REQUIRED SALES
Original	$0.40	$250,000	$150,000	$1,000,000
Decrease selling prices	$0.25	$250,000	$150,000	$1,600,000
Advertise	$0.40	$300,000	$150,000	$1,125,000

You are being provided with three choices, all of which could potentially deliver $150,000 profit:

* Trade on a contribution of $0.40 per $1 sale, spend $250,000 on store running costs, and target sales at $1,000,000
* Reduce contribution to $0.25 per $1 sale (through lower selling prices), still spend $250,000 on store running costs, but increase the sales target to $1,600,000
* Increase store running costs by $50,000 (by advertising), trade on a contribution of $0.40 per $1 sale, and increase the sales target to $1,125,000

What you now need to do is decide which, if any, of the strategies is achievable. It is important to note that although CVP analysis can greatly simplify the decision-making process when devising sales strategies, it does not make the decision for you. Ultimately, it is still down to you to decide which of the strategies is achievable.

Why do businesses fail to make a profit?

Using CVP analysis to evaluate potential sales strategies will often highlight possible trading problems, thus enabling them to be addressed long before they ever become an issue. Some of the more common pitfalls companies fall into are detailed below.

* **Fixed costs too high**
  Day-to-day operating costs, which are often fixed in nature, are allowed to grow to an unsustainable level. Subsequent sales turn out to be insufficient to cover this high fixed cost base.
* **Fixed costs too low**
  A fear of overspending results in day-to-day operating costs being contained at levels where the business is unable to service its customers effectively. This will have an adverse affect on trading, resulting in sales being insufficient to cover even the low fixed cost base.
* **Prices too high**
  Prices are set high, either to generate a high profit on each sale or to cover what is perceived as a high fixed cost base. Customers are deterred from buying what they regard as expensive goods and services, which has an adverse effect on profit performance.
* **Prices too low**
  Prices may be lowered to stimulate sales. However, small decreases in prices often require large increases in sales to compensate for the lower profit achieved on each sale. The additional sales achieved may be insufficient to compensate for the lower profit being earned on each sale, resulting in falling profits overall.
* **Profit targets too high**
  Setting profit targets that are unattainable may demotivate staff, which will have an adverse effect on trading performance.

✳ **Profit targets too low**

Although a company may report profit every year, the level of profit being achieved may be insufficient to justify the level of funding provided by the investors. This could result in the subsequent sale or even closure of the business.

Many of these problems can be avoided if the company takes time to assess the viability of its sales plans at the outset.

 The bare bones
Many businesses fail because they do not produce commercially sound sales plans from the start.

Stripping it down to basics...

CVP analysis enables sales strategies to be assessed. Rather than beginning with a sales forecast that will inevitably involve a significant amount of guesswork, it turns the problem on its head and identifies the minimum level of sales that are necessary for a strategy to work. The technique provides three distinct benefits: it is simple to apply, it makes decision making straightforward, and it enables alternative scenarios to be evaluated. It may also help avoid a common cause of failure in many businesses – failure to produce commercially sound sales plans at the outset.

13 HOW DO YOU MANAGE PROFIT?

There's a hefty tome in your intray. On the front cover a picture of an aardvark stands resplendent. Just below this appear the words 'Aardvark Trading – Monthly Management Pack – Period 4.' The purpose of this document, as you are regularly reminded by your finance team, is to help you manage profit performance more effectively. It provides you with 'a summary of the month's trading activities,' so you should be able to make decisions that will help ensure the company achieves its profit target for the year.

As usual, you start to flick through the pages of sales and cost data looking for the key issues. Also as usual, you get confused. There are trading results for the current month, the previous month, the quarter to date, and the year to date. There are budgeted figures for the current month, the previous month, the quarter to date, the year to date, and also the full year. There are forecasts for the current quarter, the half year, and the full year. You are also told about differences between these numbers: the difference between actual trading and budgeted trading, the difference between actual trading and forecasted trading, and the difference between budgeted trading and forecasted trading. To help clarify matters these differences are quoted in both dollars and as percentages. The truth is, no matter how often you wade through this report, it never seems to make any sense. Maybe it's because you never spend enough time studying it.

This month you have resolved that things are going to be different. You have set aside an entire afternoon to review the contents. It does not take long to identify the problem. In your hands is a report that is 120 pages long with, you estimate, an average of approximately 300 figures on each page. That means you are trying to digest no fewer than 36,000 statistics and, let's not forget, this is the monthly summary! How can you possibly make any sense out of this amount of information?

Fortunately, profit management does not demand the ability to digest and analyze pages and pages of numbers. It is a great shame that when producing management information, many businesses place too much emphasis on information and not enough emphasis on management. Profit management is all about identifying the figures that count and acting on them. The objective is to identify the pertinent issues fast, thereby facilitating swift and effective decisions.

This is a large chapter – profit management is a large topic. It is well worth your time working through it, though. The real problem with profit management is that it is a subject that is littered with misconceptions. If you don't understand the principles thoroughly you can spend time investigating problems that do not exist and making decisions that will ultimately damage profit performance. Understanding this topic will save you time: it will direct you to the real problems confronting the business and highlight where management action will prove to be most beneficial. **In this chapter we are going to look at how to use sales and cost information to ensure that profit targets are achieved.**

What can you learn from a budget report?

The most common method used to report sales and cost information within a business is in the form of a budget report. As was noted in Chapter 10 ('How do you create a financial plan?'), the function of a budget is to help managers make decisions that ensure the business achieves its commercial goals, the most important of which is invariably a profit target. This is facilitated by providing budget reports that compare actual trading results achieved during a period with budgeted performance for the same period. The period under consideration may be a week, a month, a quarter, or whatever other period is deemed appropriate. The differences between actual and budgeted results are called 'variances,' which are used to indicate where managers may need to take action. In order to understand how this is achieved, we need to look at how the information is presented. A typical budget report is shown below.

REEDERM AND WEEPE INC.
BUDGET REPORT – PERIOD 1

	ACTUAL	BUDGET	VARIANCE		
	$	$	$		%
SALES	1,500,000	1,000,000	500,000	F	50 F
Cost of sales	680,000	400,000	280,000	A	70 A
GROSS PROFIT	820,000	600,000	220,000	F	37 F
Sales & marketing costs	400,000	300,000	100,000	A	33 A
Administration costs	170,000	100,000	70,000	A	70 A
OPERATING PROFIT	250,000	200,000	50,000	F	25 F

TYPICAL BUDGET REPORT

The level of detail provided in budget reports varies considerably between businesses, but the general layout tends to be reasonably consistent. Typically managers are presented with the section of the overall company's income statement for which they are responsible. If they are in a sales-related area, they are provided with an analysis of sales and cost performance. If they are in a non-sales-related area (e.g. an information technology department), they are provided solely with an analysis of costs. Regardless of the information provided, the figures reported can usually be divided into three broad categories:

* **Actual results**
  The actual trading results for the period.
* **Budgeted results**
  The planned trading results for the period.
* **Variances**
  The differences between the actual and the planned trading results.

What can we learn from these figures? It is the variance column that is commonly the focus of attention, so we need to develop a full understanding of what this set of figures is telling us.

The first point to note when examining variances is that they can be expressed either in monetary terms or as a percentage of the budgeted figure. For example, when looking at sales performance for Reederm and Weepe, it can be seen that actual sales were $1,500,000 while budgeted sales were $1,000,000. There are two ways to express this difference. We can either say that sales were $500,000 over budget or that they were 50% over budget.

This begs a question: Which type of variance is more important, dollars or percentages? The answer is always dollars. In the budget report shown on the previous page, the company has overspent on sales and marketing costs by 33% and on administration costs by 70%. Based on percentages, administration costs should be the priority. However, let's not forget that the objective of the budget is to help the company achieve a profit target, which is expressed in dollars. The only way we can deviate from this goal is through dollar variances. In this circumstance, remember the following adage:

Dollars pay bills – percentages pay nothing.

The overspend on sales and marketing costs is reducing profit by $100,000, whereas the overspend on administration costs is reducing profit by only $70,000. As a result, management should initially be directing its attention toward sales and marketing costs, because these are having the greatest impact on profit performance. This does not mean that we should not look at administration costs; all we are saying is that sales and marketing costs should be regarded as a higher priority.

 The bare bones
When examining variances, attention should be focused on the monetary variance, not the percentage variance.

The magnitude of a variance is not the only issue of concern. The direction of the variance is also relevant. In other words, is actual performance better or worse than budgeted performance? This can be the source of immense confusion. Suppose a company is currently over budget in terms of sales performance. It would normally be argued that this is good for business. Does it follow that it is good to be over budget on costs as well?

One convention that is encountered in practice to distinguish between variances is the use of plus (+) and minus (−) signs. This often does nothing more than heighten the confusion that already exists. For example, when looking at a cost variance, does a minus sign preceding it indicate that actual expenditure is less than budgeted expenditure, or does it indicate that budgeted expenditure is less than actual expenditure? Depending on the company, it could mean either!

The important issue when looking at a variance is to determine how it is affecting profit performance. After all, it is profit we are trying to manage here. In order to remove any ambiguity, we are going to adopt the following convention when looking at variances in this chapter:

F This denotes a favorable variance – it is having a favorable impact on profit performance.
A This denotes an adverse variance – it is having an adverse impact on profit performance.

Let's return to the budget report introduced earlier. Concentrating on the dollar variances, the points in the table opposite can be noted.

Combining these variances, netting off the favorable variances against the adverse variances, explains why there is a $50,000 favorable variance in operating profit.

Why does actual profit differ from budgeted profit?

By examining the reported variances for Reederm and Weepe, we can see that sales are over budget, having a favorable effect on profit, while all costs are over budget, having an adverse effect on profit. This tells us how actual operating profit turned out to be $50,000 more

ITEM	VARIANCE	INTERPRETATION
Sales	$500,000 F	Sales are $500,000 over budget, having a favorable impact on profit
Cost of sales	$280,000 A	Cost of sales is $280,000 over budget, having an adverse impact on profit
Sales and marketing	$100,000 A	Sales and marketing costs are $100,000 over budget, having an adverse impact on profit
Administration	$70,000 A	Administration costs are $70,000 over budget, having an adverse impact on profit

than budget, but it does not tell us why. How does this help management? All the report has really told us is the obvious: if sales go up, costs tend to go up. Also, all this information is historic: it is telling us what has happened in the past. Surely the report would be far more useful if it could help us decide what to do in the future.

This is the real role of a budget – it should be helping us manage future trading. Being able to use a budget to help us control the business in the future is known as 'budgetary control.' Let's return to the original budget report (reproduced overleaf).

The fundamental problem with this report is that, in its current format, it is comparing actual performance (when sales are $1,500,000) against a budget that tells us what to expect when sales are lower (at $1,000,000). All that can be deduced is that costs will be different when sales are different, but we could have worked that out without even seeing the figures!

When looking at this report, what is the most obvious question an investor would want answered? In all probability it would be this:

REEDERM AND WEEPE INC.
BUDGET REPORT – PERIOD 1

	ACTUAL	BUDGET	VARIANCE		
	$	$	$		%
SALES	1,500,000	1,000,000	500,000	F	50 F
Cost of sales	680,000	400,000	280,000	A	70 A
GROSS PROFIT	820,000	600,000	220,000	F	37 F
Sales & marketing costs	400,000	300,000	100,000	A	33 A
Administration costs	170,000	100,000	70,000	A	70 A
OPERATING PROFIT	250,000	200,000	50,000	F	25 F

BUDGET REPORT – REVISITED

＊ **Why is actual profit different from budgeted profit?**

As a manager, you want to be able to provide the answer. In addition, you want to identify where action is required. A technique called 'variance analysis' allows you to do this. It is designed to answer the three most common questions encountered when dealing with budgets:

＊ **Why is actual profit different from budgeted profit?**
＊ **Where is management action required?**
＊ **How is management action to be prioritized?**

The easiest way to understand this technique is to see how it is applied in practice.

The bare bones
Variance analysis addresses three issues:
   ＊   **Understanding why profit changes**
   ＊   **Identifying where action is required**
   ＊   **Deciding how to prioritize action**

When a profit plan has been created, there are two classes of variance that can subsequently arise:

* **Sales variances**
* **Cost variances**

Sales variances arise when sales deviate from budget, whereas cost variances arise when costs deviate from budget.

A word of advice: Variance analysis is used extensively in the business world. Regrettably, people can find some of the concepts and associated calculations hard to grasp. As a result, you may find it beneficial to read the rest of this section slowly. This will be time well invested, because if you can get to grips with this technique you will have a powerful management tool at your disposal.

Let's start by looking at sales variances. Sales in Reederm and Weepe are $500,000 higher than budget. Is this necessarily a good thing? Shareholders will not be impressed if a company announces that it has increased sales by 50% but profit has remained unaltered. It follows when examining sales that what we are really interested in is the profit earned on those sales; that is, gross profit. So when looking at the sales figures for Reederm and Weepe, rather than spending time on why they have increased, what we really want to know is why the gross profit on those sales is $220,000 more than budget. Variance analysis asks how this latter situation could possibly arise.

There are only two ways any business can make more gross profit:

* **It sells more goods and services**
* **It makes more gross profit per $1 sale**

This has led to the identification of two types of sales variance:

* **Sales volume variance**
  This tells us by how much gross profit has changed due to the volume of sales changing
* **Sales margin variance**
  This tells us by how much gross profit has changed due to the percentage gross profit on sales changing

Let's look at how each of these variances is calculated.

Given that a sales volume variance is concerned with the impact of changing sales on profit, it is logical to start by establishing by how much sales have changed from plan:

	$
Actual sales	1,500,000
Budgeted sales	1,000,000
Difference in sales	500,000

Having established that sales are $500,000 above budget for the period, what we now want to know is how much additional gross profit should be generated as a result. In order to address this, we need to re-examine the budget report. According to the budget, on sales of $1,000,000 the company was expecting to make $600,000 gross profit, which can be expressed as a percentage:

$$\text{Budgeted gross profit as a percentage of sales} = \frac{\text{Budgeted gross profit of \$600,000}}{\text{Budgeted sales of \$1,000,000}} \times 100\%$$

$$= 60\%$$

So the company planned to make 60% gross profit on its sales. It follows that if sales are $500,000 above budget, 60% of this figure should be gross profit:

	$
Difference in sales	500,000
x Budgeted gross profit as a percentage of sales	x 60%
Sales volume variance	300,000 F

This is a sales volume variance. It tells us that, given sales are $500,000 above budget, gross profit should be $300,000 above budget. In order to establish this, we have performed two calculations. In practice, these can be combined into one calculation (which obviously provides the same result):

	$
Actual sales	1,500,000
Budgeted sales	1,000,000
Difference in sales	500,000
x Budgeted gross profit as a percentage of sales	x 60%
SALES VOLUME VARIANCE	300,000 F

CALCULATING A SALES VOLUME VARIANCE

We can now draw our first key conclusion: given that sales are above budget, gross profit should have increased by $300,000. However, the operating profit of the company is only $50,000 above budget, so other things must be taking place that are affecting overall profit performance.

Apart from volumes changing, the only other way sales can affect profit is if the percentage gross profit achieved on those sales alters. This is a sales margin variance. To calculate this, we start off by establishing how much gross profit we should be earning on actual sales achieved. This can be readily established by multiplying actual sales by the budgeted percentage gross profit on sales (which we have already worked out as being 60%):

	$
Actual sales	1,500,000
x Budgeted gross profit as a percentage of sales	x 60%
Expected gross profit	900,000

Given sales of $1,500,000, we should expect to be making $900,000 gross profit. To establish the sales margin variance, we compare this with the gross profit we have actually made:

	$
Expected gross profit	900,000
Actual gross profit	820,000
Sales margin variance	80,000 A

This is a sales margin variance. It tells us that the percentage gross profit on sales is less than planned, resulting in actual gross profit being $80,000 below what we would have expected, given current sales of $1,500,000. As with the sales volume variance, we can combine the two-stage approach we have just adopted into one calculation:

	$
Actual sales	1,500,000
x Budgeted gross profit as a percentage of sales	x 60%
Expected gross profit	900,000
Actual gross profit	820,000
Sales margin variance	80,000 A

CALCULATING A SALES MARGIN VARIANCE

When combined, the sales volume variance and the sales margin variance explain why gross profit differs from budget by $220,000:

Sales volume variance of $300,000 F
combined with
Sales margin variance of $80,000 A
explains the
Gross profit variance of $220,000 F
(as quoted in the budget report)
Note: Favorable and adverse variances can be offset against each other.

We are now in a position to answer the question: 'Why is gross profit $220,000 more than budget?'

✳ Sales are $500,000 higher than planned, which should result in gross profit being $300,000 more than budget
✳ But the percentage gross profit earned on those sales is lower than planned, thereby reducing potential gross profit by $80,000.

We can now see why this technique is called variance analysis. It takes the raw variance from the budget report and breaks it up into new variances that explain why the difference arose in the first place.

Let's summarize what we have learned about sales variances. Gross profit is a combination of the volume of sales achieved and the percentage gross profit achieved on those sales:

Gross profit = Volume of sales x Percentage gross profit achieved
on those sales

A sales volume variance identifies how gross profit is affected when the volume of sales alters. A sales margin variance identifies how gross profit is affected when the percentage gross profit achieved on sales alters.

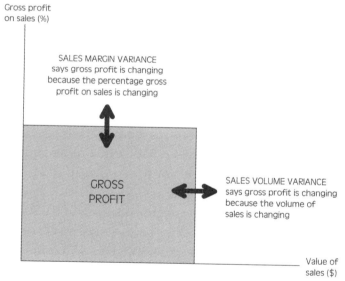

SALES VARIANCES EXPLAIN CHANGES IN GROSS PROFIT

Having explained why gross profit achieved on sales has changed, we now need to turn our attention to costs and understand how they are affecting profit. Starting with sales and marketing costs, it can be seen from the budget report for Reederm and Weepe that these are $100,000 above budget. There are only two possible reasons for a cost to increase:

* Sales increase thereby increasing costs
* More is being spent to achieve a $1 sale

This has led to the identification of two types of cost variance:

* **Cost volume variance**
  This tells us by how much a cost has changed due to the volume of sales changing
* **Cost rate variance**
  This tells us by how much a cost has changed due to the rate of spend on each $1 sale changing

Let's look at how to calculate a cost volume variance for sales and marketing costs. What we want to know is what impact changing sales are having on costs. This is facilitated by comparing the budgeted cost with what the cost should now be given current sales. It follows that we need two figures:

* **Budgeted cost**
  This is obtained direct from the budget report, i.e. $300,000.
* **What the cost should now be**
  This is the tricky bit! We can see from the budgeted figures that the company planned to spend $300,000 on sales and marketing costs to achieve $1,000,000 worth of sales. In other words, sales and marketing costs were planned to be 30% of sales. It follows that if we had known sales were going to be $1,500,000 when the budget was being set, sales and marketing costs would have been planned at 30% of $1,500,000, i.e. $450,000.

We are now in a position to calculate the cost volume variance for sales and marketing costs.

	$
Budgeted cost	300,000
What the cost should now be	450,000
Sales and marketing volume variance	150,000 A

CALCULATING A COST VOLUME VARIANCE FOR SALES AND MARKETING COSTS

Given that sales are $500,000 above budget, we would have expected sales and marketing costs to increase by $150,000, which will adversely affect profit. Note that although this is an adverse variance, it does not mean that managers have done anything wrong – this is a justifiable increase in expenditure. However, it is an increase in expenditure and that is why an adverse variance is reported.

The only other way costs can change is if productivity alters. In other words, more or less is being spent to achieve a $1 sale. This is a cost rate variance. To calculate this, we compare the actual cost with what the cost should now be given current sales. By looking at the budget report, we can see that actual expenditure on sales and marketing is $400,000. We have also established we would expect the cost to be $450,000, given current sales of $1,500,000. The cost rate variance is the difference between these two figures.

	$
Actual cost	400,000
What the cost should now be	450,000
Sales and marketing rate variance	50,000 F

CALCULATING A COST RATE VARIANCE FOR SALES AND MARKETING COSTS

Expenditure on sales and marketing is $50,000 less than we would have expected, given current sales of $1,500,000.

We can combine these two cost variances to explain why sales and marketing costs differ from budget.

Sales and marketing volume variance of	$150,000 A
combined with	
Sales and marketing rate variance of	$50,000 F
explains the	
Sales and marketing variance of	$100,000 A
(as quoted in the budget report)	

We can now answer the question: 'Why are sales and marketing costs $100,000 above budget?'

* Sales are $500,000 higher than planned, which should result in an increase in sales and marketing costs of $150,000
* But the rate of spend per $1 sale on sales and marketing costs is less than planned, thereby reducing expected expenditure by $50,000

Turning our attention to administration costs, exactly the same approach is adopted as that used with sales and marketing costs. We can divide the administration cost variance in the budget report into a cost volume variance and a cost rate variance.

We calculate the cost volume variance for administration costs in the same way as we did for sales and marketing costs. We compare the budgeted cost with what the cost should now be given current sales. As previously, we need two figures:

* Budgeted cost
  This is obtained direct from the budget report, i.e. $100,000.
* What the cost should now be
  The budgeted figures tell us that the company planned to spend $100,000 on administration costs to achieve $1,000,000 worth of sales. That is to say, administration costs were planned at 10% of sales. Given current sales of $1,500,000, it is logical to expect administration costs to be 10% of this figure, i.e. $150,000.

We can now calculate the cost volume variance for administration costs.

	$
Budgeted cost	100,000
What the cost should now be	150,000
Administration volume variance	50,000 A

CALCULATING A COST VOLUME VARIANCE FOR ADMINISTRATION COSTS

Given that sales are $500,000 above budget, we would have expected administration costs to increase by $50,000.

The cost rate variance for administration costs also adopts a similar approach to that adopted for sales and marketing costs. We compare the actual cost with what the cost should now be given current sales. The budget report tells us that expenditure is $170,000. We have already established that the cost should be $150,000 given current sales of $1,500,000. The cost rate variance is the difference between these two figures.

	$
Actual cost	170,000
What the cost should now be	150,000
Administration rate variance	20,000 A

CALCULATING A COST RATE VARIANCE FOR ADMINISTRATION COSTS

Expenditure on administration costs is $20,000 more than we would have expected, given current sales of $1,500,000.

By combining the volume and rate variances, we can establish why administration costs differ from budget.

Administration volume variance of	$50,000 A
combined with	
Administration rate variance of	$20,000 A
explains the	
Administration variance of	$70,000 A
(as quoted in the budget report)	

This places us in a position to answer the final question that is pertinent to the budget report of Reederm and Weepe: 'Why are administration costs $70,000 more than budget?'

* Sales are $500,000 higher than planned, which should result in an increase in administration costs of $50,000
* Plus the rate of spend per $1 sale on administration costs is more than planned, resulting in a further increase in costs of $20,000

Let's summarize what we have learned about cost variances. Any cost incurred by a business can be viewed as a combination of the volume of sales achieved and the rate of spend per $1 sale:

Total cost = Volume of sales x Cost per $1 sale

A cost volume variance identifies how a cost is affected when the volume of sales alters. A cost rate variance identifies how a cost is affected when the rate of spend per $1 sale alters.

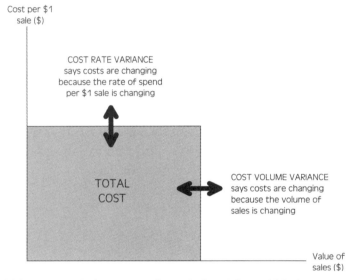

COST VARIANCES EXPLAIN CHANGES IN TOTAL COSTS

Having calculated all the relevant variances, we are now in a position to answer the first question that variance analysis is designed to address:

✳ **Why is actual profit different from budgeted profit?**

This can be tackled directly by preparing a document known as an 'operating statement,' which reconciles budgeted profit performance to actual profit performance. Although there are various ways in which this can be presented, typically the first figure that appears at the top of the report will be the budgeted profit for the period, while the last figure shown at the bottom of the report will be the actual profit achieved. In the case of Reederm and Weepe, the objective of the operating statement is to explain why actual operating profit is $250,000 while budgeted operating profit is $200,000.

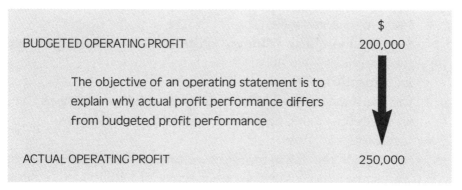

	$
BUDGETED OPERATING PROFIT	200,000
The objective of an operating statement is to explain why actual profit performance differs from budgeted profit performance	
ACTUAL OPERATING PROFIT	250,000

THE OBJECTIVE OF AN OPERATING STATEMENT

We can explain why actual performance differs from budgeted performance by inserting the variances previously calculated.

REEDERM AND WEEPE INC.
OPERATING STATEMENT – PERIOD 1

			$	$
BUDGETED OPERATING PROFIT				200,000
Sales	Volume	300,000 F		
	Margin	80,000 A		
TOTAL SALES VARIANCES				220,000 F
EXPECTED OPERATING PROFIT (after sales variances)				420,000
Sales & marketing	Volume	150,000 A		
	Rate	50,000 F		
Administration	Volume	50,000 A		
	Rate	20,000 A		
TOTAL COST VARIANCES				170,000 A
ACTUAL OPERATING PROFIT				250,000

A TYPICAL OPERATING STATEMENT

Let's examine this document line by line.

* **Budgeted operating profit**
  The company planned to make an operating profit of $200,000 during the period.
* **Sales volume variance**
  Sales are more than planned, which should result in increased gross profit of $300,000.
* **Sales margin variance**
  The percentage gross profit earned on sales is lower than planned, thus reducing potential gross profit by $80,000.
* **Total sales variances**
  Netting off the favorable sales volume variance of $300,000 against the adverse sales margin variance of $80,000 tells us that the combined effect of increased sales and falling margin has still resulted in an increase in overall profit of $220,000.
* **Expected operating profit (after sales variances)**
  Given that sales variances have increased profit by $220,000, it follows that operating profit should increase by the same amount from its budgeted level of $200,000 to $420,000. This is assuming that operating costs have not altered from plan. Since actual operating profit for the period is less than $420,000, it follows that costs must be affecting profit as well.
* **Sales and marketing volume variance**
  Given that sales are more than planned, sales and marketing costs should have increased by $150,000.
* **Sales and marketing rate variance**
  Productivity has improved (for every $1 sale, less is being spent on sales and marketing than planned), which has reduced expected expenditure by $50,000.
* **Administration volume variance**
  Given that sales are more than planned, administration costs should have increased by $50,000.
* **Administration rate variance**
  Productivity has deteriorated (for every $1 sale, more is being spent on administration than planned), which has increased expected expenditure by $20,000.

* **Total cost variances**

  Offsetting the favorable against the adverse cost variances, costs account for a decrease in profit of $170,000.
* **Actual operating profit**

  Given that cost variances are decreasing profit by $170,000, this explains the difference between the expected operating profit (after sales variances) of $420,000 and the actual operating profit of $250,000.

The bare bones
An operating statement reconciles budgeted profit to actual profit.

Variance analysis is a powerful tool that enables us to understand why variances exist between actual and budgeted results. There are alternative methods for calculating variances, but the versions shown here are the ones that tend to be the most appropriate for managers, since they have the advantage of being reasonably straightforward to calculate while still imparting valuable management information.

Where is management action required?

By preparing an operating statement, we have been able to answer the first question that variance analysis is designed to address: 'Why is actual profit different from budgeted profit?' That is the hard bit out of the way! Answering the second question this technique is designed to address is far more straightforward:

* **Where is management action required?**

By examining the variances in the operating statement above, we can readily identify areas of concern. In Reederm and Weepe, there are two:

* The sales margin variance indicates that there may be a problem with the margin as the percentage gross profit being earned on

sales is less than planned. This may be due to decreased selling prices, increases in the direct costs of the goods and services sold, or a change in the sales mix (proportionately more low-margin sales are taking place than planned).
* The administration rate variance indicates that there may be a problem with cost control, as more is being spent than planned on administration costs per $1 sale.

Note that although the sales and marketing volume variance and the administration volume variance are both adverse, these are justifiable overspends. We would expect these costs to go up because sales have increased.

How is management action to be prioritized?

We are now in a position to answer the third question that variance analysis is designed to address:

* **How is management action to be prioritized?**

By stating all variances in monetary terms, we are able to prioritize issues. In the budget report for Reederm and Weepe we have identified two issues: the percentage gross profit being achieved on sales and the rate of spend on administration costs. We can now rank these in terms of priority.

1 **The falling percentage gross profit on sales. This is currently losing the company potential profit of $80,000.**
2 **The increased rate of spend per $1 sale on administration costs. This is currently losing the company potential profit of $50,000.**

Although we are focusing attention here on issues that are having an adverse effect on profit, it is equally important to examine the issues that appear to be having a favorable effect on profit. For example, the favorable sales and marketing rate variance indicates that expenditure per \$1 sale is less than budgeted. If this has been achieved by reducing staffing levels, it might be that staff morale is being affected, which could have adverse effects on trading in the future. Alternatively, if this improvement has been achieved by finding a more effective way of deploying this expenditure, this might be a strength that could be exploited further.

How should you use a budget report?

Let's summarize how to use variance analysis when examining a budget report. It can be viewed as a four-stage process:

STAGE 1
Calculate a sales volume and a sales margin variance to explain the difference between budgeted and actual gross profit

STAGE 2
For each cost below the gross profit line, calculate a cost volume and a cost rate variance to explain the difference between the budgeted and the actual cost

STAGE 3
Prepare an operating statement incorporating all the variances identified in Stages 1 and 2

STAGE 4
Using the operating statement, identify and prioritise required management action

Failure to adopt this approach can lead to managers drawing misleading conclusions and pursuing inappropriate action. Let's revisit the budget report of Reederm and Weepe.

REEDERM AND WEEPE INC.
BUDGET REPORT – PERIOD 1

	ACTUAL	BUDGET	VARIANCE	
	$	$	$	%
SALES	1,500,000	1,000,000	500,000 F	50 F
Cost of sales	680,000	400,000	280,000 A	70 A
GROSS PROFIT	820,000	600,000	220,000 F	37 F
Sales & marketing costs	400,000	300,000	100,000 A	33 A
Administration costs	170,000	100,000	70,000 A	70 A
OPERATING PROFIT	250,000	200,000	50,000 F	25 F

BUDGET REPORT – REVISITED

We will now compare what this report tells us with what variance analysis says (see table opposite).

The original budget report suggests that there are two issues adversely affecting profit: the overspend on sales and marketing costs and the overspend on administration costs. Out of these, the overspend on sales and marketing costs should take priority because it represents the largest overspend. Note that the overspend on cost of sales is not perceived as a problem as gross profit is still above budget.

Variance analysis also suggests that there are two issues adversely affecting profit: the decreased percentage gross profit being achieved on sales and the increased rate of spend per $1 sale on administration costs. Of these, the decreased percentage gross profit on sales is deemed the most important, as this is having the greatest monetary impact on profit. In fact, variance analysis goes on to suggest that sales and marketing costs are not a problem at all. If anything, we should be trying to ascertain how the company has managed to reduce its expenditure per $1 sale and congratulate those responsible for this improvement in performance!

Comparing the original budget report with the results of variance analysis highlights a very important issue. The original budget report

	CONCLUSION DRAWN FROM BUDGET REPORT	CONCLUSION DRAWN FROM VARIANCE ANALYSIS
SALES	Sales are $500,000 above budget	Increased sales should increase gross profit by $300,000 above budget
Cost of sales	Cost of sales is $280,000 above budget, indicating a possible cost management issue	Percentage gross profit on sales is less than planned, thereby reducing potential gross profit by $80,000
GROSS PROFIT	Gross profit is $220,000 above budget, suggesting the overspend on cost of sales is not a critical issue	
Sales and marketing costs	Sales and marketing costs are $100,000 above budget, indicating a possible cost management issue	The rate of spend per $1 sale is lower than planned. resulting in costs being $50,000 less than expected (given current sales of $1,500,000)
Administration costs	Administration costs are $70,000 above budget, indicating a possible cost management issue	The rate of spend per $1 sale is higher than planned, resulting in costs being $20,000 more than expected (given current sales of $1,500,000)
OPERATING PROFIT	Operating profit is $50,000 above budget	Operating profit is $50,000 above budget

should never be used in its raw form to determine where management action is required.

REEDERM AND WEEPE INC. BUDGET REPORT – PERIOD 1			VARIANCE	
				%
SALES			00,000 F	50 F
Cost of sales			80,000 A	70 A
GROSS PROFIT			20,000 F	37 F
Sales & market			00,000 A	33 A
Administration			0,000 A	70 A
OPERATING PROFIT	250,000	200,000	50,000 F	25 F

DO NOT USE RAW BUDGET REPORTS TO DETERMINE MANAGEMENT ACTION

The original budget report tells you where variances exist. However, you need variance analysis to explain why these variances have arisen. Until you have established the reasons for variances existing, it is impossible to identify any required action. This explains why variance analysis is such an important technique: it can save management considerable time by ensuring that attention is dedicated to genuine management issues and not wasted trying to resolve issues that do not exist in the first place.

The bare bones

When examining budget reports, always use variance analysis to identify where action is required – the original report can be very misleading.

Stripping it down to basics...

Managing profit demands an ability to identify where action is required. Variance analysis facilitates this by addressing three issues: understanding why profit changes, identifying where action is required, and prioritizing issues. This is achieved by focusing attention on monetary (as opposed to percentage) variances and why they arise.

A sales variance can be broken down into two elements: a sales volume variance and a sales margin variance. A cost variance can also be broken down into two elements: a cost volume variance and a cost rate variance. These can all be brought together in an operating statement, which reconciles budgeted profit to actual profit.

Failure to analyze variances and why they arise, and instead focusing attention on budget reports in their raw form, can result in attention being directed to issues that do not exist and a failure to identify the issues that are important.

14 WHAT ABOUT CASH FLOW?

You can now appreciate that profit management is about balancing costs against sales and that the reason you need profit is to provide a return to shareholders. You can also appreciate that cash flow is not the same thing – but when it comes to managing the business, is the management of cash flow really that different from the management of profit?

The current mantra in your company is: 'We must improve cash flow!' Your colleagues tell you that this is just another way of saying that the company wants more profit: 'If sales increase, more cash will flow into the company. If costs are reduced, less cash will flow out of the company.' In response to the current call for improved cash flow, it has been suggested more generous payment terms should be offered to customers enabling them to settle their invoices over a longer period. The general consensus is that this will promote sales activity and, as everybody knows, more sales will ultimately result in more cash flowing into the business. Despite the intuitive appeal of this argument, the finance division is strongly opposed to the idea, arguing that it will adversely affect cash flow! This suggests that profit management and cash management are definitely not the same thing.

Regrettably, it is the inability to distinguish profit management from cash management that has led to the downfall of many a business. Even as you read these pages, some companies are focusing all their attention on profit performance and completely neglecting cash flow. They do so at their peril. Ironically, the most common cause of business failure is not the inability to make profits (there are thousands of companies every day that report losses), it is the inability to generate cash flow. **In this chapter we are going to establish how cash management differs from profit management and how it can be assessed.**

What is cash management?

In Chapter 3 ('How do you make profit?') we saw how making profit is a process that can be broken down into a series of discrete stages:

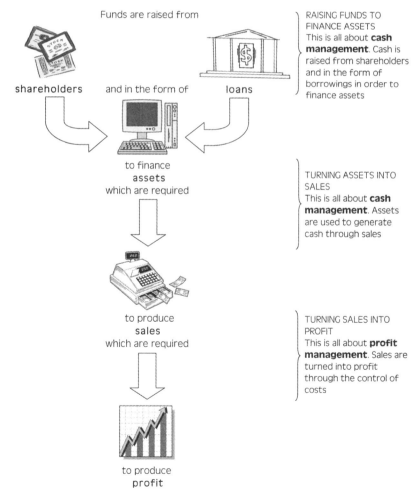

Funds are raised from

RAISING FUNDS TO FINANCE ASSETS
This is all about **cash management**. Cash is raised from shareholders and in the form of borrowings in order to finance assets

shareholders   and in the form of   loans

to finance
assets
which are required

TURNING ASSETS INTO SALES
This is all about **cash management**. Assets are used to generate cash through sales

to produce
sales
which are required

TURNING SALES INTO PROFIT
This is all about **profit management**. Sales are turned into profit through the control of costs

to produce
profit

THE PROFIT-MAKING PROCESS

The first two stages of the profit-making process focus on cash management: raising cash to finance assets and using these assets to generate cash in the form of sales. It is only the final stage that is true profit management: turning sales into profit. A feature that is common to the first two stages is the presence of assets – the first stage is about financing assets while the second stage is about utilizing them. If a business invests cash in assets from which it is unable to generate cash in the form of sales, it will be unable to meet its expenses. This is why cash management is so important. As a result, when we talk about cash management, what we are really talking about is asset management.

Assets are normally divided into two types: fixed and current. Fixed assets are assets that are intended to be maintained in their current form for more than one year, whereas current assets are expected to be consumed or turned into another form within the next 12 months. As a general rule, when companies declare that they want to improve cash flow, they tend to be looking for an immediate improvement. Given that fixed assets tie up cash for a long period, their ability to generate cash also tends to be spread over a long time. Consequently, when companies are looking for an improvement in cash flow, it is current assets (which by their nature are short term) that tend to be the focus of attention. However, in order to get to grips with cash management, you need to understand a new concept: 'net current assets' (which is also sometimes referred to as 'working capital'). To explain this we need to return to the profit-making process.

According to this process, the more assets a business needs the more funds it has to raise to finance those assets. The problem with raising additional funds from shareholders is that additional profit will be required to provide an adequate rate of return on those funds. The problem with borrowing funds is it can commit the business to onerous interest payments. Of course, if it were possible to borrow funds without having to pay any interest, borrowing would not be an issue. This is not an idle fantasy – it can be done.

Our study of the balance sheet earlier in this book indicated that it was common practice to divide liabilities into two types:

✳ **Long-term liabilities**
Amounts owed that are payable after more than one year.

Although there are exceptions, the bulk of long-term liabilities tends to be long-term borrowing on which interest is payable.

✳ **Current liabilities**

Amounts owed that are payable within one year. In essence, this is short-term borrowing and the great news is that in many instances there is no interest to be paid.

By managing current liabilities effectively, it is possible to raise additional finance for a company without the need to increase profit for shareholders or pay any more interest on loans. Some of the more common sources of short-term finance that a company can obtain are detailed overleaf.

As you can see, most types of short-term finance can be obtained without the need to pay any interest. The one exception tends to be short-term finance raised from banks, but even this only commits the company to paying interest in the short term. The significance of short-term sources of finance lies in the fact that they reduce the need to raise long-term finance from shareholders or in the form of long-term borrowings.

Net current assets refers to the proportion of current assets that need to be financed by long-term funds. To calculate this we deduct current liabilities from current assets – whatever is left over needs to be financed by long-term funds:

Net current assets = Current assets – Current liabilities

Suppose that a company has current assets of $25 million and current liabilities of $15 million. In this instance, current assets are being financed by two sources:

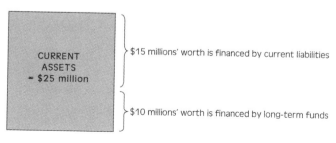

CURRENT ASSETS = $25 million

$15 millions' worth is financed by current liabilities

$10 millions' worth is financed by long-term funds

SOURCE	SHORT-TERM FINANCE PROVIDED	COST TO THE COMPANY
Suppliers	A company can obtain short-term finance from its suppliers by agreeing to pay for goods and services after they have been received. For example, a company may agree to pay its suppliers 30 days after delivery takes place	Nil
Staff	A company can obtain short-term finance from its staff by agreeing to pay them at the end of the week or at the end of the month	Nil
Government	A company can obtain short-term finance from the government, as taxes do not usually have to be paid until after the end of the period to which they relate	Nil
Banks	A company can obtain short-term finance from a bank, e.g. by requesting an overdraft facility	Interest

So $10 millions' worth of current assets need to be financed by long-term funds. This can be raised either from shareholders (who will demand profit to provide a rate of return on their investment) or in the form of borrowings (on which interest will need to be paid each year). By minimizing net current assets, the company takes pressure off its profit figure and its interest commitments. Cash management is all about keeping net current assets to a practical minimum, but without adversely affecting trading.

What is the link between
cash management and profit management?

Let's revisit the profit calculation and examine how it relates to the creation of net current assets.

PROFIT CALCULATION   IMPACT ON NET CURRENT ASSETS

Profit in a period

= Sales in a period   When credit is offered to customers, this
                               leads to the creation of a current asset, i.e.
                               accounts receivable

LESS Costs incurred   When goods have to be bought in or
to produce that period's   manufactured for resale, this leads to the
sales   creation of a current asset, i.e. **inventory**
                               When credit is obtained from suppliers,
                               this leads to the creation of a current
                               liability, i.e. **accounts payable**

THE RELATIONSHIP BETWEEN PROFIT AND NET CURRENT ASSETS

As you can see, there are three direct links between the profit calculation and net current assets:

✳ Accounts receivable

When a company offers credit to customers, although the sale may take place today there may be a delay of several weeks before the customer hands over the cash. This creates accounts receivable (amounts owed by customers), which is a form of current asset. The greater the level of credit offered to customers, the greater the funding required to finance this delay in receiving cash.

✳ **Inventory**

When goods are being sold this often creates the need for inventory to be maintained within the business, which is another form of current asset. The greater the level of inventory being carried, the greater the funding required to finance it while awaiting sale.

✳ **Accounts payable**

When short-term credit is obtained from suppliers this creates accounts payable, which is a form of current liability. In other words, it provides a source of short-term funding that can be used at least partially to finance current assets. The more short-term funding that is obtained, the less long-term funding that needs to be raised.

Note that the profit calculation is unaffected by any of these issues. Whether customers pay cash on delivery or on credit, the sales figure is unaffected. Whether inventory levels being carried are high or low, reported costs are unaffected. Whether or not credit terms are obtained from suppliers, reported costs are again unaffected. These issues only affect cash flow and it is they that form the core elements of cash management within any business.

 The bare bones

The term 'cash management' usually refers to the management of net current assets – the difference between current assets and current liabilities.

How can you measure cash performance?

Cash management is all about time management. When you are managing cash, what you are in fact managing is a period of time. This is the time that elapses between handing cash out to suppliers and receiving cash back from customers. The shorter this period is, the better will be your cash flow. Technically, this period of time is known as the 'cash cycle.'

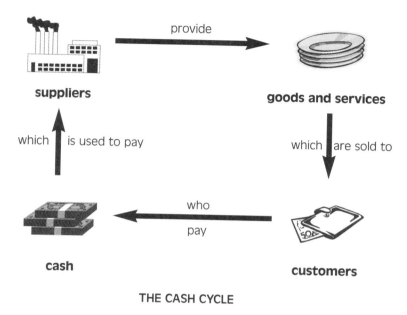

THE CASH CYCLE

There are four stages in the cash cycle:

* **Suppliers provide goods and services**
  If payment is made to suppliers on receipt of goods and services, cash leaves the business as soon as deliveries take place. However, if credit terms can be obtained from suppliers, the business will enjoy the benefit of goods and services received without having to release cash immediately, which will have a favorable effect on cash flow.
* **Goods and services are sold to customers**
  Inevitably, there will be a delay between the receipt of goods and services and subsequent sales. When dealing specifically with goods, the longer this delay, the more cash that is being tied up in inventory, which will have an adverse effect on cash flow.
* **Customers pay cash**
  If payment is demanded from customers on delivery of goods and services, cash will be received as soon as sales take place. However, when credit terms are offered to customers, the receipt

of cash is being deferred. The longer it takes to receive payment, the more cash that is effectively being loaned to customers, thus having an adverse effect on cash flow.

✳ **Cash is used to pay suppliers**

The gap between having to pay suppliers and receiving cash from customers is the cash cycle. Ideally most businesses would like to receive cash from customers before paying suppliers, but in practice few businesses manage to achieve this.

The objective of cash management in most businesses is to minimize the cash cycle. This is tantamount to minimizing net current assets. Examining the flowchart on the previous page, the cycle starts with suppliers providing goods and services, after which there are three distinct time periods:

✳ **The time between receiving goods and services and selling them to customers**
✳ **The time between making sales to customers and receiving the cash**
✳ **The time between suppliers providing goods and services and having to pay the cash**

The cash cycle is calculated by combining these three elements:

Cash cycle = Time that elapses between the delivery of **inventory** and its subsequent conversion into sales

PLUS Time that elapses between the sale of goods and services to customers and the receipt of monies due from these **accounts receivable**

LESS Time that elapses between the receipt of goods and services from suppliers and subsequent payment to these **accounts payable**

The longer inventory sits in the business awaiting sale, the longer will be the cash cycle. It will be extended further if credit is offered to customers. It follows that increasing inventory levels and extending credit offered to customers will have an adverse effect on cash flow as more cash is tied up in net current assets. The good news is that the cash cycle can be shortened by obtaining credit from suppliers. When this happens, for a while at least, the suppliers are helping to finance the business.

Note that the cash cycle focuses attention on credit obtained from suppliers. This does not mean that other forms of short-term finance are not important. Being able to defer payment to any third party (the government, staff, or whoever) will always have a favorable effect on cash flow.

Suppose a company buys inventory from a supplier on four weeks' credit; that is, the amount due must be settled within four weeks from delivery. On average, it takes ten weeks to sell the inventory and customers are given eight weeks to settle their accounts. The cash cycle would be as follows:

Cash cycle = Time that elapses between the delivery of **inventory** and its subsequent conversion into sales (10 weeks)

      PLUS Time that elapses between the sale of goods and services to customers and the receipt of monies due from these **accounts receivable** (8 weeks)

      LESS Time that elapses between the receipt of goods and services from suppliers and subsequent payment to these **accounts payable** (4 weeks)

      = 10 weeks + 8 weeks – 4 weeks

      = 14 weeks

The company has to wait 14 weeks between handing cash out to its suppliers and receiving cash back from its customers. The shorter this period, the better will be the cash flow.

So far we have assumed a business that is trading in goods. What if the business only provides a service? In this circumstance, there is no inventory being carried and the cash cycle contracts to just two components:

Cash cycle = Time that elapses between the sale of services to customers and the receipt of monies due from these **accounts receivable**

     LESS Time that elapses between the receipt of goods and services from suppliers and subsequent payment to these **accounts payable**

The bare bones

The objective of cash management is to minimize the time that elapses between paying cash to suppliers and receiving cash from customers.

Is there an optimal cash flow?

Based on our discussion so far, some people might conclude that an optimal cash flow exists when the cash cycle is nil. In this situation, a business is paying cash to its suppliers at the same time as it is receiving cash from its customers, resulting in no cash being invested in current assets at all. A welcome situation indeed! However, there are businesses that enjoy a negative cash cycle. In other words, they receive cash from their customers before they pay their suppliers. These businesses would argue that they would like their cash cycle to be as negative as possible.

What sort of businesses can achieve a negative cash cycle? One example that is often cited is supermarkets. Suppose a supermarket typically takes on average a week to sell stock after delivery, all sales are for cash, and payment terms for suppliers are four weeks. This would result in the following cash cycle:

Cash cycle = Time that elapses between the delivery of **inventory** and its subsequent conversion into sales (1 week)

     PLUS Time that elapses between the sale of goods and services to customers and the receipt of monies due from these **accounts receivable** (Nil – payment terms are cash on delivery)

     LESS Time that elapses between the receipt of goods and services from suppliers and subsequent payment to

these **accounts payable** (4 weeks)

= 1 week + 0 weeks − 4 weeks

= −3 weeks

Cash is being received from customers three weeks before it has to be paid to suppliers. The company has no cash invested in current assets – they are all being financed by the suppliers. In this situation, the supermarket would be keen to make its cash cycle as negative as possible. This is because the more negative the cash cycle, the more cash will be provided by suppliers to finance other assets (i.e. fixed assets) within the business, thus enabling it to grow. Consequently, in many supermarkets suppliers are not just financing the inventory they supply, they are also helping to finance the store!

The bare bones
A negative cash cycle provides two benefits:
* **No long-term funds are needed to finance current assets**
* **Suppliers are providing funds to finance fixed assets**

Stripping it down to basics...

Cash flow is critical to business success. When businesses refer to cash management, they are usually referring to the management of net current assets – balancing current assets against current liabilities. The objective is to minimize the cash cycle, the time that elapses between paying cash to suppliers and receiving cash from customers. If a negative cash cycle can be achieved without adversely affecting trading, this has two benefits: no long-term funds are needed to finance current assets, plus suppliers are providing funds to finance fixed assets.

15 HOW DO YOU MANAGE CASH FLOW?

Every manager knows that cash flow is important and is keen to improve it. However, wanting something is not the same as achieving it. Understanding cash flow is a skill set in itself, but what you really want to know is how to improve it. What practical actions do you need to take?

The management of cash flow is based on a few readily understandable principles. **In this chapter we are going to look at how to manage the key issues that can affect cash flow performance.**

What are the main issues that affect cash flow?

As discussed in Chapter 14, at the heart of cash flow is the cash cycle, management of which can be divided into three broad categories:

* **Inventory management**
  Minimize the time that elapses between the delivery and subsequent sale of inventory
* **Accounts receivable management**
  Minimize the time that elapses between making a sale and receiving payment from the customer
* **Accounts payable management**
  Maximize the time that elapses between receiving goods and services from suppliers and making the associated payments

The intention is to achieve each of these objectives, but without jeopardizing sales and (most importantly) profits. This raises three questions:

* How do you manage inventory?
* How do you manage accounts receivable?
* How do you manage accounts payable?

How do you manage inventory?

The management of accounts receivable involves collecting monies due from customers as promptly as possible. The management of accounts payable involves maximizing the use of available credit terms offered by suppliers. The objective in both cases is clear. However, what is the objective of inventory management? Is it simply to carry as little inventory as possible? In many businesses, if they tried to do this such a strategy may well result in lost sales – not a desirable situation! Inventory management demands a more subtle approach.

When looking at inventory levels, what we are really interested in is how effectively these are being utilized to generate sales. This can be assessed using a measure called 'stockturn' (or 'inventory turn'). This tells us how many times stock (or inventory) is turned over during a predefined period, typically a year.

Suppose a photographic business buys and sells 12,000 cameras during a year. One way to run the business would be to buy 12,000 cameras at the beginning of the year and then sell them over the next 12 months. This would result in the business turning over its inventory once during the year – it would have a stockturn of 1. This raises a question: does the business need 12,000 cameras at the beginning of the year? Could it still achieve the same sales if it only started off the year with 1,000 cameras, bringing in another 1,000 in the second month, another 1,000 in the third month, and so on? Note that in both scenarios the business is still buying and selling 12,000 cameras. However, in the latter scenario it will turn over its inventory 12 times during the year, producing a stockturn of 12. This results in cash only being tied up in 1,000 cameras at the start of the year, compared with

12,000 cameras in the original scenario. This will free up considerable amounts of cash that can be utilized elsewhere in the business to develop profits further. We can conclude from this that the objective of inventory management is to achieve maximum stockturn without impairing sales performance.

Another way of looking at stockturn is as a rate of return. The higher the stockturn, the more sales are being achieved during a year, relative to the amount of cash that is tied up in inventory. When viewing stockturn this way, it is evident that the most bizarre question you could ask any business is: 'What stockturn would you like to achieve?' This is equivalent to asking someone what rate of return they would like to earn on their savings. Anybody in their right mind would want the highest rate of return possible!

This brings us to an important point. Stockturn is a historical measure. It is there to tell us how we have done – it is not a planning tool. Its importance stems from the fact that if stockturn can be improved, the return to shareholders will improve (since less funds will be tied up in inventory to achieve the same level of profit). The problem with this measure is that it cannot tell us if inventory is moving too quickly (resulting in missed sales opportunities) or too slowly (implying excessive inventory levels).

Stockturn can be likened to a speedometer on a car. A speedometer is very good at telling you how fast you are traveling. What it cannot do is tell you whether you should speed up or slow down – you need completely different information to make this decision. In order to evaluate and plan inventory levels, a different measure is required.

 The bare bones
Stockturn is a historical measure that indicates how fast inventory is being turned over. It is not a planning tool.

'Forward cover' measures the time that elapses between taking delivery of inventory and its ultimate sale. Let's return to the photographic business. Suppose it is achieving a stockturn of 12: it is turning its inventory over 12 times a year. To achieve this, it follows that on average it must be turning over its inventory once a month. Another way of saying the same thing is that it takes an average of one month for inventory to move through the business from the point of delivery to the point of sale.

This principle provides a powerful planning aid. If a business wants to achieve a stockturn of 12, it could do so by consistently ordering sufficient inventory to cover the next month's sales. Hence the title: forward cover. Stock should be ordered to cover future sales. It follows that the faster inventory is being turned over, the shorter will be the forward cover being maintained. Logically, there is a unique forward cover associated with any stockturn. Here are just a few examples:

ANNUAL STOCKTURN	FORWARD COVER
1	1 year
2	6 months
3	4 months
4	3 months
5	2.4 months (approximately 10 weeks)
6	2 months

If a business is achieving a stockturn of 1, it is taking a year to move inventory through the business, whereas if it is achieving a stockturn of 6, it is only taking two months to move inventory through the business. The higher the stockturn, the shorter the period during which inventory is tying up cash. In this respect, the following adage is worth remembering:

Dead inventory equals dead cash.

The appeal of forward cover is that it is intuitive. Suppose a company is achieving a stockturn of 3. Is this good or bad? It's hard to say. However, a stockturn of 3 is equivalent to a forward cover of four months. To say it takes four months to move inventory is far easier to visualize. It has already been pointed out earlier in this chapter that the question that should never be asked in relation to inventory is 'What stockturn would you like to achieve?' The question that should be asked is: 'What forward cover can you survive on?' To answer this, the required forward cover can be assessed by reference to four factors:

* **Supplier lead times**
  The time until the next delivery of inventory determines the minimum forward cover that is required. For example, if it is three weeks until another delivery can be expected, at least three weeks' forward cover is required to ensure that inventory is available to support sales.
* **Uncertain sales**
  The more uncertainty there is surrounding anticipated sales, the greater will be the tendency to carry additional inventory 'just in case'. This will result in increased forward cover.
* **Minimum order size**
  If suppliers insist on imposing minimum order sizes, a business may have to carry more forward cover than it would like. Smaller, more frequent deliveries are one way to reduce forward cover. This should be balanced against the discounts that might be lost by no longer making bulk purchases.
* **Minimum display requirements**
  Some businesses such as retailers need inventory for display purposes. The more inventory that is required to be on display, the greater will be the forward cover.

Returning to the photographic business, suppose deliveries take place every four weeks. This means that at least four weeks' worth of cameras would be needed after each delivery to ensure that inventory does not run out before the next intake. However, what would happen if there were more customers than expected in the meantime? This would result in lost sales unless there was enough inventory to satisfy this unexpected increase in demand. Consequently, the business might decide to carry an extra two weeks' cover. In addition, in order to maintain a reasonable display, it might decide to carry a further week's cover. This would result in the business planning to carry sufficient inventory to cover the next seven weeks' worth of sales after each delivery.

The bare bones
Inventory levels in a business should be planned and assessed on the basis of forward cover.

To close this particular topic, it is worth mentioning a concept that is often raised in relation to inventory – the 'just-in-time' principle. Why is this discussed so much? In reality, the answer is simple – it's the only inventory principle most people have ever heard of! It says that inventory should be delivered just as it is about to be utilized. This is merely another way of saying that a business would like to maintain a forward cover of nil. Although this is a theoretical ideal, since no cash would be tied up in inventory, for many businesses it is not practical.

The environment in which just in time is most commonly quoted is manufacturing. Ideally, a manufacturer would like stocks of raw materials and consumables to arrive as they are about to be used in the production process. Even in this situation, though, what would happen if there was a sudden increase in demand and associated production requirements? In a retail business, how would stores look if merchandise was delivered as it was about to be sold? Empty stores are not conducive to sales. As a result, although nil forward cover is an attractive proposition, it is only practical in very rare cases. However, businesses should still strive to minimize forward cover, but with the caveat that they should not jeopardize sales.

How do you manage accounts receivable?

When credit is offered to customers, the time that elapses between paying suppliers and receiving payment from customers is extended. In other words, the cash cycle is extended. Of course, the reason businesses offer credit terms to customers is to stimulate sales. Bear in mind that when offering credit terms, a company is effectively offering free finance. This benefit must be balanced against the adverse effect it is having on cash flow.

Consequently, a measure has been devised to assess how effectively accounts receivable are being managed. 'Debtor days' refers to the average number of days it takes to collect sums owed from customers. For example, if debtor days is 45, this means that on average 45 days elapse between raising the invoice on a customer and receiving payment. Obviously, the shorter this period is, the better the cash flow will be.

Two strategies that would improve debtor days are as follows:

* **Only offer sufficient credit terms to achieve a sale**
  Offering credit terms that are in excess of customer expectations
  results in needlessly extending the cash cycle
* **Maintain tight credit control over customer debts**
  Once credit terms have been agreed with a customer, ensure that
  payment is received when it falls due. Lax credit control will lead
  to an unnecessary extension of the cash cycle.

The second of these strategies is the most common cause for
debtor days being excessively long. Companies will go to great lengths
to negotiate prompt payment terms, even offering discounts. However,
once the invoice is raised, they place insufficient emphasis on ensuring
that customers adhere to these terms.

The bare bones
**Debtor days measures how effectively customer credit is
being managed.**

Accounts receivable only exist when companies offer credit terms
to customers that they intend to finance themselves. Some industries
offer extended payment terms where the finance is provided by a third
party. For example, retailers often accept payment by credit card.
Alternatively, the customer may be asked to sign a credit agreement,
which is, in fact, a contract with a third party (typically a bank). In both
cases, the credit card company or the bank pays the full amount due to
the company within days of the transaction taking place. The customer
is then obliged to pay back the credit card company or the bank the
sum involved (plus interest). This results in the customer receiving
extended payment terms, but without jeopardizing the cash flow of the
retailer. It is when no third party is involved that offering credit terms
to customers adversely affects cash flow, since the company will not
receive cash until the customer makes payment.

How do you manage accounts payable?

Obtaining credit from suppliers has the opposite effect on cash flow to extending credit to customers. The longer the credit period obtained from suppliers, the better will be the business's cash cycle. It should come as no surprise that, just as a measure exists that comments on how effectively customer credit is being managed, there is a measure that comments on how effectively supplier credit is being managed. 'Creditor days' refers to the average number of days it takes to pay sums owed to suppliers. For example, if creditor days are 60, this means that on average 60 days elapse between the supplier raising an invoice and payment being made. The longer this period is, the better the cash flow will be.

This would seem to suggest that companies should endeavor to maximize payment periods with suppliers. However, this should not be pushed too far, as it might adversely affect future trading. Three arguments are commonly put forward to support this view:

* **The supplier might refuse to supply**
  The supplier might refuse to continue to supply the business if payment terms are perceived as onerous.
* **The supplier might increase prices**
  The supplier could take the view that extended payment terms are a form of loan and will build a finance charge into future prices.
* **The supplier might go bankrupt**
  Particularly when dealing with smaller suppliers, if payment is delayed how will the supplier pay its own bills in the meantime? This could result in the supplier going bankrupt, which would obviously not be of benefit to either business.

For these reasons, many businesses take the view that although extending payment terms to suppliers can significantly reduce the cash cycle, there are practical limits to how far this policy can be pursued. As a result, many prefer to negotiate discounts with their suppliers in return for prompt payment. This enables the supplier to maintain a healthy cash cycle, while the company can enjoy improved profit margins.

The bare bones
Creditor days measures how effectively supplier credit is being managed.

Should companies maintain high or low cash balances?

So far we have identified three strategies to enhance the cash cycle:

* **Increase stockturn**
* **Reduce debtor days**
* **Increase creditor days**

Pursuing one or more of these strategies will reduce the cash cycle, thereby freeing up cash. This will only be of benefit, though, if when the cash is released it is subsequently utilized. One of the worst things a company can say to its shareholders is that it is 'cash rich' or has a 'cash mountain.' This implies that there are large amounts of cash doing nothing. The only reason shareholders invest cash in a business is for it to be put to work, not for it to sit around in a bank account. Consequently, large cash balances should be:

* **Either reinvested back into sales-generating assets**
* **Or handed back to investors (e.g. in the form of dividends)**

This highlights an important point – healthy cash flow and high cash balances are not the same thing.

* **Healthy cash flow**
  means having enough cash flowing into the business to pay the expenses as they arise. This should result in very low cash balances being maintained throughout the year. Telling shareholders their cash is being utilized and working hard for their benefit is a positive message to send out.

* **High cash balances**

  implies large sums of money not being utilized. This is definitely not a good message to send out to shareholders.

Stripping it down to basics...

Cash management is improved if a business's cash cycle can be shortened. Three strategies exist for reducing the cash cycle: increase stockturn, reduce debtor days, and increase creditor days. Stockturn can be maximized by planning and managing inventory levels on the basis of forward cover, endeavoring to keep this to a minimum. Debtor days can be minimized by collecting monies due from customers promptly. Creditor days can be maximized by taking advantage of payment terms available from suppliers.

Any cash released by such initiatives must not be left idle – it should either be reinvested back in the business or handed back to the investors.

16 WHAT ABOUT LONG-TERM PROJECTS?

On the one hand the company wants payroll costs to be cut back and yet, at the same time, it is quite happy to spend millions of dollars on a new computer system. It seems to be making up the rules as it goes along. It ought to make a definitive statement – either it is trying to reduce costs or it is not.

As we shall discover, long-term projects (such as investing in a computer system) always demand special treatment. Regrettably, the rules that apply to managing normal day-to-day expenses do not apply in this instance. **In this chapter we are going to determine why long-term projects are a special case and what decision-making process needs to be undertaken when deciding whether or not to invest in them.**

What is a long-term project?

A long-term project can be defined as an initiative that requires the outlay of cash now with the intention of either increasing future revenue or reducing future expenditure, where the benefit is expected to extend over more than one year.

With very few exceptions, projects that fall within this definition tend to involve the acquisition of fixed assets, which by their very nature are assets expected to be maintained in their current form for more than a year. This immediately sets this type of decision apart from other types of expenditure. Most expenses are short term in nature. Inventory, payroll, utility bills, equipment hire charges, and so on tend to be paid on a regular basis and are expected to yield benefits in the immediate future. If too much is spent on these cost categories, action can be taken quickly to remedy the situation.

Fixed assets are different. If a business invests in a fixed asset that turns out to be non-productive, it may prove to be far more difficult to resolve the issue. Suppose several million dollars is invested in machinery that has been custom built to manufacture disposable televisions – watch them once then throw them away! If demand for this product does not materialize (which seems likely), the business is left with an unproductive asset. To compound the problem, its resale value (given that it's a customized piece of equipment) will probably be close to its scrap value. It follows that very careful consideration needs to be paid to any such proposed expenditure.

Before proceeding any further, we need to make an important cost distinction. In Chapter 11 ('How do you manage costs?') we noted that expenditure in a business can be divided into fixed costs and variable costs. An alternative way of dividing expenditure is as follows:

* **Capital expenditure**
  This refers to the acquisition or improvement of fixed assets. In other words, this is expenditure that will yield a benefit over more than one year.
* **Revenue expenditure**
  This refers to day-to-day operating expenses. This would include items such as inventory, payroll, rent, and so on. Consequently, this is expenditure that will yield a benefit in the short term (where short term in this context means within one year).

Overleaf are a few examples of what would be classed as revenue expenditure and what would be classed as capital expenditure.

REVENUE EXPENDITURE	CAPITAL EXPENDITURE
Purchase of stationery	Purchase of furniture
Maintenance of computer equipment	Purchase of computer equipment
Purchase of raw materials	Purchase of manufacturing equipment
Purchase of petrol and oil	Purchase of vehicles
Rent of property	Purchase of property

Deciding whether or not to acquire a fixed asset or indulge in any other type of long-term project can be broken down into three stages:

* **Argue the case**
* **Evaluate the risk**
* **Make the accept/reject decision**

The first stage demands that a sound commercial argument be prepared to justify the proposed project. Unfortunately, no matter how appealing such an argument may appear, every proposal faces a problem – it is dealing in the future and nobody knows for certain what the future holds. As a result, every proposal has an element of risk attached to it. Consequently, the second stage in the decision-making process is to assess the risk. Finally, if the commercial argument is deemed reasonable and the associated risk appears to be within acceptable limits, the final stage is to decide whether or not to proceed.

In this chapter we are going to focus attention on the first two stages and the next chapter discusses the accept/reject decision.

Argue the case

Assess the risk

Make the decision

EVALUATING A LONG-TERM PROJECT COMPRISES THREE STAGES

How do you argue the case for a long-term project?

When considering a long-term project, the first issue that needs to be addressed is what information should be included in the argument and what information should be left out. Obviously, the anticipated benefits must be included. However, when considering the costs, a strict commercial rule applies: attention must be confined to 'relevant costs.' This might seem an obvious comment. After all, who would want to include irrelevant costs? However, 'relevant costs' is a piece of financial jargon with a very precise definition:

* **A relevant cost is defined as a future cash outflow that results directly from the decision under consideration**

According to this definition there are three criteria that must be satisfied if a cost is to be included in the argument. Let's revisit the definition, but this time highlighting the key words:

* A relevant cost is defined as a **future cash** outflow that results directly from the **decision** under consideration

We can examine the significance of each of the key words in turn:

* **Future**

Only future cash flows are to be taken into account. Past expenditure must be ignored. Suppose a business has fixtures currently sitting unused in a warehouse. A new project is being proposed that could utilize these. Should the cost of these fixtures be included as a cost of the project? The answer is no – the expenditure has already taken place. No new cost will be incurred if they are used in the project. Indeed, if they are not used, this will result in assets remaining dormant, which is clearly of no benefit to the business at all.

* **Cash**

Most long-term projects involve a significant outlay of cash at the outset. Consequently, the argument should concentrate on cash flow. Suppose equipment is to be purchased. The purchase price of the equipment would be a relevant cost (because cash will be moving out of the business), but depreciation on the equipment would not be a relevant cost (because when depreciation takes place, there is no physical movement of cash).

✱ **Decision**

We are only interested in cash that will move as a direct result of the decision under consideration. If the business is already committed to spending cash, regardless of the decision being considered, it is not relevant. Suppose a business wants to introduce a new computer system and it intends using a printing press (which it already rents) to produce operating manuals for the system. Should an apportionment of the rental costs be included as a relevant cost? Although any additional stationery and labor costs would be relevant (since these costs will only be incurred if the project proceeds), the rental of the printing press will take place regardless of what happens with the project. Consequently, the rental costs are not relevant and should not be included in the proposal.

The bare bones

When arguing a case for a long-term project, attention must be confined to the anticipated benefits and the associated relevant costs.

Having identified the appropriate figures, these should be tabulated (typically year by year) for the entire life of the project. This is sometimes called a 'cost–benefit analysis' and details all the costs and benefits associated with a project.

Sparky Electronics wants to invest in new production equipment and has identified the following benefits and associated relevant costs:

✱ The purchase price of the equipment will be $300,000 and the project is expected to last three years

✱ Increased sales of $500,000 each year are expected to result

✱ Additional cost of sales (raw materials and other direct costs of production) are expected to be $320,000 per annum

✱ Additional operating costs (administration, marketing and so forth) are expected to be $50,000 per annum

These can be summarized in the form of a cost–benefit analysis.

	YEAR 0 $	YEAR 1 $	YEAR 2 $	YEAR 3 $	TOTAL $
BENEFITS					
Additional sales		500,000	500,000	500,000	1,500,000
COSTS					
Equipment	–300,000				–300,000
Cost of sales		–320,000	–320,000	–320,000	–960,000
Operating costs		–50,000	–50,000	–50,000	–150,000
NET CASH FLOW	–300,000	130,000	130,000	130,000	90,000

A COST–BENEFIT ANALYSIS

Let's examine what this cost–benefit analysis is saying to us. You will note that there is a column entitled 'Year 0.' This is common practice and it simply means 'right now.' In other words, it refers to revenue or expenditure that will arise at the outset. In this instance, the only immediate cash flow will be the purchase of the equipment for $300,000.

Now let's turn our attention to the benefits. Based on the information provided, there is only one type of benefit: additional annual sales of $500,000. Against this, we must offset the additional annual costs comprising cost of sales of $320,000 and operating costs of $50,000. So during each of the three years of the project's life, there will be a net cash inflow of $130,000.

In summary, we have an initial cash outflow of $300,000 followed by three net annual cash inflows of $130,000, providing the business with $90,000 more cash at the end of the project than at the start.

Just because a project generates $90,000 additional cash over its life, it does not follow that it is a worthwhile investment. Unfortunately, the project may be nowhere near as appealing as may at first appear. This is because all the figures presented are based on estimates of future trading performance. Given that nobody actually knows what the future holds, it follows that there must be an element of risk involved. Consequently, before deciding whether or not to proceed, we need to evaluate the project's risk.

How do you evaluate the risk of a long-term project?

Let's be clear what we mean by risk:

* Risk can be defined as the possibility of a future outcome arising that will produce adverse results.

Every decision in business involves an element of risk. Fortunately, many decisions are short term in nature and numerous opportunities exist to correct a problem should it arise. However, when dealing with decisions where the impact may span several years, the opportunities to correct an adverse outcome may be far more limited. Consequently, the assessment of risk is far more pertinent when dealing with this latter type of decision.

One of the most commonly used methods to assess risk is called 'sensitivity analysis' and the reason for its popularity is that it is relatively straightforward to apply. However, despite its simplicity, it is powerful in terms of what it can tell you. It assesses risk by examining how the outcome of a proposed strategy will change if an assumption changes. The more sensitive the outcome of a project is to the assumptions being made, the higher the risk.

For example, sensitivity analysis can be used to answer questions such as the following:

* What will happen to anticipated profit if sales are 5% below plan?
* What will happen to anticipated profit if estimated payroll costs are 10% above plan?
* What will happen to anticipated profit if equipment supplier prices are 15% above plan?

To gain an understanding of how this technique works, we are going to address the following question:

* How wrong can the assumptions made about a project be before it is no longer profitable?

The objective of most long-term projects is to increase profits in the future. If you rush into the boardroom screaming 'I've identified a great investment opportunity that won't generate any profit at all!' don't be surprised if you are invited to leave the room fairly promptly.

The bare bones

Sensitivity analysis evaluates the risk of a long-term project by assessing how sensitive the anticipated outcome is to the assumptions being made.

Let's return to the cost–benefit analysis for Sparky Electronics.

	YEAR 0 $	YEAR 1 $	YEAR 2 $	YEAR 3 $	TOTAL $
BENEFITS					
Additional sales		500,000	500,000	500,000	1,500,000
COSTS					
Equipment	–300,000				–300,000
Cost of sales		–320,000	–320,000	–320,000	–960,000
Operating costs		–50,000	–50,000	–50,000	–150,000
NET CASH FLOW	–300,000	130,000	130,000	130,000	90,000

COST–BENEFIT ANALYSIS – REVISITED

As noted previously, over its life the project will produce a positive net cash flow of $90,000. This does not mean it is definitely worth investing in, but it is worthy of consideration. The one thing we can be certain of is that if net cash flow is zero (i.e. there is no perceived commercial benefit), interest in the project will also be zero. Unfortunately, the projected net cash flow at the end of the three years is based on assumptions about sales and cost performance – assumptions that may well turn out to be wrong. What we need to establish is how wrong these assumptions can be before the project is no longer profitable.

Before we do this, it is important to note that when we refer to 'profit' in this context, we are referring to net cash flow (i.e. by how much cash inflows exceed cash outflows). At first sight this might seem to contradict what we established very early in this book, that profit and cash flow are very different concepts. However, long-term projects are a special case. The objective here is to start with a pile of cash and end up with a larger pile of cash at the end of the project. In other words, it is being assumed that the only asset you start off with is cash and the only asset you end up with is cash. In this unique situation, profit does equal net cash flow. In this example, we start off with $300,000 cash but end up with $390,000 cash (comprising three annual net cash inflows of $130,000 each), providing a net cash inflow of $90,000.

Let's begin by looking at the purchase price of the equipment. The question that needs to be addressed is this:

* **By how much can the cost of the equipment increase before the project is no longer profitable?**

If the cost of the equipment turns out to be $90,000 more than expected, this would wipe out the forecasted net cash inflow of $90,000. This provides us with our first conclusion:

* **If the cost of the equipment increased by 30% above plan (from $300,000 to $390,000), the project would no longer be profitable.**

Now let's move on to cost of sales and ask a similar question:

* **By how much can the cost of sales increase before the project is no longer profitable?**

The approach to answering this question is identical to that adopted in the case of the equipment. Bearing in mind that the projected net cash inflow over the life of the project is $90,000, it follows that if cost of sales turns out to be $90,000 above plan, profit would be reduced to nil. This gives us our second conclusion:

* **If cost of sales increased by 9.4% (from $960,000 to $1,050,000), the project would no longer be profitable.**

The same approach is adopted when looking at operating costs:

✳ **By how much can the operating costs increase before the project is no longer profitable?**

Once again, if this cost increased by $90,000, the project would no longer be profitable. This provides us with another conclusion:

✳ **If operating costs increase by 60% (from $150,000 to $240,000), the project would no longer be profitable.**

Having examined the costs of the project, let's move on to the estimated benefits – the additional sales. The issue here is slightly more intricate because it does not follow that if they turn out to be $90,000 below plan, the project will make zero profit. This is due to the fact that if sales fall, some costs will fall as well. This does mean that a little more work will be needed to establish how sensitive the project is to sales changes.

Fortunately, a formula exists to help resolve this issue. In fact, the really good news from our point of view is that this is a formula we have already encountered in Chapter 12 ('How do you manage sales?') – long-term projects are a perfect application for CVP analysis. Let's remind ourselves of how this technique works. It all rotates around a formula, the objective of which is to identify the sales required for a strategy to work:

$$\text{Required sales} = \frac{\text{Planned fixed costs} + \text{Planned profit}}{\text{Planned contribution per \$1 sale}}$$

where
Fixed costs are costs that remain unaffected by changes in sales
Contribution per $1 sale is the profit made on a $1 sale after only paying for variable (sales-related) costs

In the case of Sparky Electronics, the cost of the equipment will not change regardless of what happens to sales. Also, in many businesses operating costs tend to be primarily fixed in the short term. This means that total fixed costs over the life of the project will be $450,000 (comprising $300,000 cost of equipment plus $150,000 operating costs). Turning our attention to the required profit in the formula, this needs to be set at nil since we are trying to identify what sales will result in profit falling to zero.

The only other figure we need to establish is the planned contribution per $1 sale. We can see from the cost–benefit analysis that projected sales over the three years are $1,500,000. Logically, the variable costs are the cost of sales because these are the direct costs of the goods being sold. These total $960,000 over the life of the project. So after paying for cost of sales, the business is left with $540,000 out of sales of $1,500,000, which is equivalent to $0.36 per $1 sale. We can now identify the sales that would result in zero profit being made:

$$\text{Required sales} = \frac{\text{Planned fixed costs} + \text{Planned profit}}{\text{Planned contribution per \$1 sale}}$$

$$= \frac{\$450,000 + \$0}{\$0.36}$$

$$= \$1,250,000$$

If sales fall to $1,250,000, the project will make nil profit. This is $250,000 less than the original plan of $1,500,000. That is, sales would need to fall by 16.7% before profit hits zero.

We are now in a position to summarize how sensitive the outcome of the project is to the various assumptions that have been made, by detailing the permitted margins of error before the project is no longer profitable:

REVENUE/COST	PERMISSIBLE MARGIN OF ERROR
Additional sales	16.7%
Equipment	30.0%
Cost of sales	9.4%
Operating costs	60.0%

So:

If sales are 16.7% less than plan or
If the cost of equipment is 30.0% above plan or
If cost of sales are 9.4% above plan or
If operating costs are 60.0% above plan

the project would no longer make a profit.

If it is believed that any of the revenue or cost estimates could be out by more than the associated margin of error, the viability of the project should be called into doubt. Indeed, this technique helps us identify the most critical issues. In this instance, the most critical issue surrounds cost of sales. If direct costs of production exceed forecast by more than 9.4%, this project will produce a loss. Is this a realistic possibility? If it is, the project should not proceed in its current form.

You should note that sensitivity analysis as described above looks at each benefit and cost individually, thereby making the assumption that all other figures shown are accurate. This has the advantage of highlighting which figures are creating the greatest risk. However, what if estimates relating to more than one of the figures turn out to be wrong?

'Cross-sensitivity analysis' examines the impact on the outcome of a project when several variables change at the same time. Referring to the above example, it could be used to answer the question: 'What happens to profit if sales are 10% below plan, equipment costs are 15% above plan, and cost of sales are 5% above plan?' The problem with this approach is that it will not tell you whether it is sales, equipment, or cost of sales that is creating the biggest impact. Not surprisingly, many businesses confine their attention to basic sensitivity analysis; that is, they examine the impact on profit of a change in one variable at a time. This is because the primary role of the technique is to get a feel for where the risk lies. In the example above, we have established that cost of sales poses the greatest threat to the success of the project and it therefore needs to be examined more closely before proceeding any further.

We have now worked our way through the first two stages of the decision-making process that relate to long-term projects:

* We have argued the case by identifying the anticipated benefits and associated relevant costs of a project, laying them
  out in the form of a cost–benefit analysis
* We have evaluated the risk of the project using sensitivity
  analysis

However, even if the risk identified for a project is deemed to be
within acceptable limits, it does not follow that we should proceed
with the initiative. This is where the final stage of the decision-making
process comes into play – making the accept/reject decision. That is the
subject of the next chapter.

Stripping it down to basics...

Long-term projects can affect trading within a business over
many years. As a result, emphasis should be placed on ensuring that
the correct decision is made at the outset. Such decisions involve three
stages: argue the case, assess the risk, and make the accept/reject
decision.

When arguing the case, attention should be confined to anticipated benefits and associated relevant costs, which can be incorporated
in a cost–benefit analysis. The risk of the project can then be assessed
using sensitivity analysis, which evaluates the risk by assessing how
sensitive the anticipated outcome is to the assumptions being made.
Only when these two stages have been completed can the accept/reject
decision be made.

17 HOW DO YOU DECIDE IF A LONG-TERM PROJECT IS WORTHWHILE?

It has taken you weeks to put together the case for a new computer system in your department. The existing one is a complete waste of time. You acknowledge that a new system will be costly, but when this is compared against the hours currently lost every week trying to resolve problems, the decision is obvious. The company is insistent that whenever a proposal is made for any major project a full analysis of all the costs and benefits be prepared. In this respect you have been extra vigilant. Not only have you managed to identify and quantify every potential cost associated with the project, you have also provided a schedule detailing all the problems you believe could potentially arise and the various contingency plans you have in place to deal with them. No matter how you look at it, the cost savings over the next few years will definitely outweigh the costs – this is surely a done deal!

For the past two weeks the finance department has been poring over your figures and this is the morning you receive their decision. The good news is that they accept your figures as showing that the future savings will clearly outweigh the costs. Then comes the bad news. The project is to be rejected for two reasons. As they so eloquently put it: 'There is no doubt that the project would increase the profits of the company. However, it has failed the IRR hurdle and the payback period is excessive. As a result, there is no alternative but to reject this proposal.'

You leave the meeting confused. On the one hand you are being told that if the project proceeded it would increase profits and yet at the same time you are being told that the company is not interested. What really frustrates you is that nobody has ever taken the time to explain what 'payback' means and you've never heard of the 'IRR hurdle.' Having spoken to your colleagues, you are not alone. Whenever major projects are submitted to the company, no matter how logical the proposal may appear, the finance department seems to view this as an opportunity to confuse people with jargon, while at the same time recommending decisions that nobody seems to understand. However, such decisions are based on sound commercial principles.

If you can get to grips with this topic, you will be held in awe by your colleagues at work, because many people believe that it involves highly technical concepts that only the most mathematically literate brain can cope with. This is not the case. The concepts, as you will discover, are remarkably straightforward and also very logical. It is true that some mathematics is involved if you want to apply the techniques we are going to examine. However, from a managerial perspective what is important is what the concepts mean and how the decisions are made. The formulae can be left to the accountants. If figures don't happen to be your thing, don't fret – skip the calculations and just make sure you understand the principles. **In this chapter we are going to review the most common methods used in practice to decide whether or not to invest in a long-term project.**

How do you make the accept/reject decision?

We noted in the previous chapter that there are three stages in evaluating a long-term project:

* Argue the case
* Evaluate the risk
* Make the accept/reject decision

When the first two stages have been completed, if the project is deemed to be commercially reasonable and the risk is within acceptable limits, we need to move on to the most critical stage in the process: the accept/reject decision. Do we proceed with the project or not?

Suppose a company adopts the following policy when it comes to deciding whether or not to approve a long-term project:

* **If a long-term project is deemed to be profitable, the risk is within acceptable limits, and it is consistent with the objectives of the business, the project will be approved.**

You would not be alone if you felt that this was an eminently reasonable policy to adopt. It may surprise you to learn, then, that most businesses would never dream of having such a policy in place. Why not? The problem is that, much as businesses would like to invest in every profitable opportunity that comes along, there is a limit to the amount of cash they have available. Deciding which projects to pursue is all about choosing how to allocate limited amounts of cash.

Central to this type of decision is a concept known as 'opportunity cost,' which ironically has nothing to do with money. Opportunity cost refers to the opportunity that will be foregone if one course of action is pursued in favor of another. If a decision is made to spend money refurbishing offices, the opportunity cost of doing this (i.e. the next best alternative) might be the sales that could have been generated by spending the money on a new customer database. This principle can be applied to help make any form of investment decision.

Imagine you want to open up an instant access savings account with a bank. Opportunity cost says that before you do this, you must determine whether or not you could earn more interest elsewhere. If you cannot, then proceed. However, if you could earn more interest elsewhere, you should not open this account. In business we need to apply the same discipline. Clearly, if a company is considering tying up substantial amounts of cash in a long-term project, it is good sense to examine what other uses the cash could be put to.

Various techniques are used to evaluate the opportunity cost of long-term projects. There are four that are commonly encountered in practice:

* **Return on investment**
* **Payback**
* **Net present value**
* **Internal rate of return**

Don't be off put by the jargon – all will be explained in the next few pages. The point to note at this stage is that the function of each of these techniques is to help businesses decide which long-term projects to invest their cash in by telling them whether or not more attractive investment opportunities exist elsewhere. Each technique has its own unique way of evaluating the opportunity cost of a project. As a result, it is down to the organization to select the technique it feels is most appropriate to its circumstances. In practice, some businesses will use just one of these techniques while others may use two, three, or even all four.

What is return on investment?

'Return on investment' (often abbreviated to ROI) is a simple concept. At its most basic level, it is designed to answer the question:

* **If cash is invested in a project, what annual percentage rate of return can be expected?**

There are various ways in which this can be worked out. A popular method is as follows:

$$\text{Return on investment} = \frac{\text{Average profit per annum}}{\text{Average value of the investment}} \times 100\%$$

 The bare bones

Return on investment provides the average annual percentage rate of return earned on funds invested in a project.

Suppose you have had a savings account for the past five years, during which time you earned $500 interest in total. Your average profit (interest) per annum is $100. However, to calculate your return on investment, we also need to know the average balance in the account over the five-year period. If the average balance was $2,000, we can work out your return on investment as follows:

$$\text{Return on investment} = \frac{\text{Average profit per annum}}{\text{Average value of the investment}} \times 100\%$$

$$= \frac{\$100}{\$2,000} \times 100\%$$

$$= 5\%$$

Your average annual rate of return is 5%. In other words, on every $100 you have invested, you have earned annual interest of $5. Exactly the same principle applies when looking at long-term projects within a business.

Let's revisit the cost–benefit analysis for Sparky Electronics introduced in the previous chapter, where the purchase of production equipment was being considered. It's reproduced overleaf for your convenience.

In order to establish the return on investment, we need to establish two figures:

* The average profit per annum
* The average value of the investment

Over the three years the project is expected to deliver a net cash inflow of $90,000, which is equivalent to an average profit of $30,000 per annum. Note that for reasons explained in the previous chapter, when dealing with long-term projects we use the terms 'profit' and 'net cash flow' interchangeably. That is the easy part of the calculation out of the way – now for the tricky bit! Working out the average value of the investment does demand some logic, so it is worthwhile reading the next few lines carefully.

	YEAR 0 $	YEAR 1 $	YEAR 2 $	YEAR 3 $	TOTAL $
BENEFITS					
Additional sales		500,000	500,000	500,000	1,500,000
COSTS					
Equipment	−300,000				−300,000
Cost of sales		−320,000	−320,000	−320,000	−960,000
Operating costs		−50,000	−50,000	−50,000	−150,000
NET CASH FLOW	−300,000	130,000	130,000	130,000	90,000

COST–BENEFIT ANALYSIS – REVISITED

At the outset, when the equipment is purchased, $300,000 is invested. However, at the end of the three years, the equipment is assumed to be valueless and will probably be scrapped. Logically, the average value of the equipment should be the mid-point between these two figures: $150,000. This can confuse people. Why do we use the average value, when it is obvious that $300,000 is being invested at the outset?

Looking at the problem intuitively might help here. Investors are providing $300,000 at the outset to purchase the production equipment. Over the next three years, sufficient sales are anticipated to repay this investment and to provide a profit as well. So although investors will have $300,000 tied up in assets initially, they should have no funds tied up in assets at the end of the three years. This is why we use the average value of funds. If you can grasp this, you have done well!

We can now work out the return on investment:

$$\text{Return on investment} = \frac{\text{Average profit per annum}}{\text{Average value of the investment}} \times 100\%$$

$$= \frac{\$30,000}{\$150,000} \times 100\%$$

$$= 20\%$$

For every $100 invested, an average return of $20 will be achieved during each year of the project.

Should the project proceed? One way this decision can be made is by comparing it with alternative projects that are competing for the same funds. Adopting this approach, it would be the project with the highest return on investment that would get the funding.

An alternative and more common approach is to set what is called a 'hurdle rate.' This is the minimum rate of return a business decides it needs from any investment opportunity. If this rate is set at 30% per annum, the above project would be rejected. Conversely, if it is set at 15%, the project would be accepted. To a large degree, the selection of a hurdle rate is influenced by three factors:

* **Return to shareholders**
   A certain rate of return needs to be achieved to satisfy investors' expectations.
* **Cost of borrowing**
   Given that many businesses borrow some of their funds, it is essential that any investment entered into using those funds provides a rate of return in excess of the cost of borrowing.
* **Risk**
   All projects involve risk and the rate of return should be chosen to compensate adequately for the risk being undertaken.

You will note that return on investment is concerned with anticipated profits. As a result, this tends to be a technique that is used by organizations where reported profits are of primary concern.

What is payback?

While return on investment is concerned with the profitability of a project, 'payback' addresses the other issue essential to commercial survival – cash flow. Payback answers a question:

* **If cash is invested in a project, how long will it be until the original investment is paid back?**

Literally, 'When do I get my money back?'

Let's return to the cost–benefit analysis for Sparky Electronics.

	YEAR 0 $	YEAR 1 $	YEAR 2 $	YEAR 3 $	TOTAL $
BENEFITS					
Additional sales		500,000	500,000	500,000	1,500,000
COSTS					
Equipment	–300,000				–300,000
Cost of sales		–320,000	–320,000	–320,000	–960,000
Operating costs		–50,000	–50,000	–50,000	–150,000
NET CASH FLOW	–300,000	130,000	130,000	130,000	90,000

COST–BENEFIT ANALYSIS – REVISITED

The initial outlay is $300,000 followed by annual net cash inflows of $130,000 for the next three years. Each of these net cash inflows helps repay the initial investment. We can tabulate this:

YEAR	NET CASH FLOW	VALUE OF INVESTMENT REPAID
Year 0	–$300,000	Nil
Year 1	+$130,000	$130,000
Year 2	+$130,000	$260,000
Year 3	+$130,000	$300,000 + $90,000 profit

At the end of Year 1, $130,000 of the original $300,000 has been repaid. At the end of Year 2, $260,000 has been repaid. At the end of Year 3, not only has the investment been paid back in full, an additional $90,000 cash has been generated as well. This suggests that the project must have paid for itself somewhere between the end of the second year and the end of the third year. Given that the project will repay itself at $130,000 per annum, it will take approximately 2 years 4 months for the initial investment of $300,000 to be repaid in its entirety. In this instance, we would say that the project has a payback of 2 years 4 months. That's all there is to payback – easy!

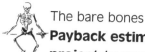 The bare bones

Payback estimates the length of time it takes for a project to pay for itself.

Whether a payback of 2 years 4 months is sufficient for the project to proceed or not can be established, as with return on investment, by comparing it against competing projects or a pre-defined target. If several projects are competing for the same funds, the one to be chosen may be the one with the shortest payback. Alternatively, if a business sets a target and demands (say) a payback within two years, the above project would be rejected. By contrast, if a payback of four years is deemed reasonable, the above project would be accepted.

To a large degree, payback periods will be influenced by the nature of the project. When looking at a long-term investment (such as buying a factory), a payback of ten years or more might be deemed acceptable. By contrast, when looking at a shorter-term investment (such as buying fixtures for a restaurant), a payback of three years or less might be deemed appropriate.

Quite often companies will demand healthy cash flow coupled with healthy profit from a project. Consequently, it is not unusual to see both return on investment and payback being used together. However, some companies use payback on its own. This means that they will invest in projects that provide a fast payback, without any reference to potential profit. Why would they be prepared to do this, given that shareholders will want a return on their investment?

As it turns out, profit is implied in payback, but it is subtly done. The logic runs as follows. In the case of Sparky Electronics, cash flows are being forecast for the next three years. Many organizations have problems forecasting over the next year, let alone three or more years. Businesses that solely look at payback argue that the longer it takes for a project to pay back, the less accurate the forecasts become. Consequently, the faster a project can pay back, the more faith can be attached to the forecasts and, most importantly, the sooner it will be generating a profit.

Notwithstanding this, most companies tend to use payback solely to assess cash flow. Consequently, it is a technique that tends to be used by companies where cash flow is deemed a critical issue.

What is net present value?

Once it's been explained most people can understand the concept of return on investment and find payback even easier to grasp. 'Net present value' (often abbreviated to NPV) seems to run on the assumption that what most businesses need is a technique that nobody will ever understand! According to return on investment and payback, if you invest $10,000 in a project and you subsequently generate a net cash inflow of $15,000, you have made a profit – well done! Surely it would confuse people if you told them you had made a loss. However, net present value may well say that this is the case. Intrigued? It should all make perfect sense in a few pages' time.

Suppose you are invited to invest $10,000 in a project and are assured you will receive $15,000 back – would you invest? Although it might sound tempting at the outset, a critical issue that needs to be clarified is when you will receive the cash. If you were told you would receive the money in 25 years' time you may well decline the offer. This is because, although you receive back $5,000 more than you invest, from your point of view $15,000 in 25 years' time is probably worth far less than $10,000 now. Net present value adopts the stance that to make a sensible decision, all cash flows should be looked at in today's terms. Hence the title 'net present value' – cash flows should be considered in present value (today's) terms.

Before we can examine how the technique works, we need to understand how to convert future cash flows into today's terms. Let's start by examining the problem intuitively. Someone asks you to lend them $1,000 for the next year and they agree to pay you back enough money to ensure you are no worse off. How would you decide how much they need to pay you back?

Most businesses would advise you to tackle the problem by looking at how much you could have earned on the $1,000 if you had invested the money elsewhere. If you could have deposited the money with a bank and earned 5% interest during the year, this would result in the bank paying you back $1,050 at the end of the 12 months (comprising the $1,000 original investment plus $50 interest). Consequently, your colleague would need to pay you at least $1,050 at the end of the year to ensure that you are no worse off. In other words, in this simple example we are saying that having $1,050 in a year's time is equivalent to you having $1,000 now.

Rather than determining intuitively what money in the future is worth now, you are probably wishing there was a formula that would do this for any amount of money at any time in the future. Good news – there is. It's called the 'discounted cash flow' (or DCF) formula. Don't worry if mathematics is not your strong point: what is relevant from a managerial perspective is understanding the results. Even so, let's take on the challenge and see if we can make sense out of this formula. Here it is:

$$\text{Present value} = \frac{\text{Future cash flow}}{(1 + \text{Rate of return})^{\text{Number of years}}}$$

This is nowhere near as bad as it looks. If you break it down into its individual components it is quite straightforward:

* **Present value**
The value of a future cash flow in today's terms. This is what we want to find out.
* **Future cash flow**
The amount of cash that is going to be received or paid out in the future.
* **Rate of return**
This is the hurdle rate. In other words, it is the annual rate of return that needs to be earned on funds to justify the investment, but expressed as a proportion. This means taking the rate of return and dividing it by 100. If the rate of return is 25% this would appear in the formula as 0.25, if the rate of return is 15% this would appear in the formula as 0.15, if the rate of return is 5% this would appear as 0.05, and so on.

✳ Number of years

The number of years in the future when the cash flow arises. This tells us what power the value in the brackets must be raised to. In other words, this tells us how many times the figure in brackets must be multiplied by itself.

The formula will probably make more sense if we look at a practical application. You are offered $1,100 in one year's time and you want to know what it is worth today. The first issue that needs to be addressed is what rate of return you could earn on funds over the next 12 months. Let's assume you could earn 10% per annum. We now have all the information we need to calculate what the cash is worth in today's terms:

* ✳ **Future cash flow** is $1,100.
* ✳ **Rate of return** is 10%. To express this as a proportion, we need to divide it by 100, which gives us 0.10.
* ✳ **Number of years** is 1. We need to wait a year for the money.

Using these figures, the discounted cash flow formula will look like this:

$$\text{Present value} = \frac{\text{Future cash flow}}{(1 + \text{Rate of return})^{\text{Number of years}}}$$

$$= \frac{\$1,100}{(1 + 0.1)^1}$$

$$= \frac{\$1,100}{1.1}$$

$$= \$1,000$$

In this instance, $1,100 in one year's time is equivalent to having $1,000 now. This is logical since, if you had $1,000 now, you could invest it at 10% per annum and you would have $1,100 in one year's time. Suppose you had to wait two years until you received the cash:

$$\text{Present value} = \frac{\text{Future cash flow}}{(1 + \text{Rate of return})^{\text{Number of years}}}$$

$$= \frac{\$1,100}{(1 + 0.1)^2}$$

$$= \frac{\$1,100}{1.1 \times 1.1}$$

$$= \$909.09$$

Based on a required rate of return of 10% per annum, $1,100 in two years' time is equivalent to having $909.09 now.

The net present value method utilizes the discounted cash flow formula to convert all future cash flows relating to a long-term project into today's terms. Let's return yet again to the cost–benefit analysis for Sparky Electronics.

	YEAR 0 $	YEAR 1 $	YEAR 2 $	YEAR 3 $	TOTAL $
BENEFITS					
Additional sales		500,000	500,000	500,000	1,500,000
COSTS					
Equipment	–300,000				–300,000
Cost of sales		–320,000	–320,000	–320,000	–960,000
Operating costs		–50,000	–50,000	–50,000	–150,000
NET CASH FLOW	–300,000	130,000	130,000	130,000	90,000

COST–BENEFIT ANALYSIS – REVISITED

The first stage in calculating the net present value of a project is to establish the hurdle rate of return. Let's assume this to be 12% per annum. The second stage of the technique requires us to summarize the net cash flows of the project year by year just as if we wanted to work out payback:

YEAR	NET CASH FLOW
Year 0	-$300,000
Year 1	+$130,000
Year 2	+$130,000
Year 3	+$130,000

Net present value says that cash in the future is not the same as cash now. Therefore, in order to make an informed judgment, all cash flows need to be converted into today's terms. This is the third stage of the technique and is achieved using the discounted cash flow formula. Based on a hurdle rate of 12% per annum, the present values of the various annual net cash flows would be as follows:

YEAR	NET CASH FLOW	PRESENT VALUE*
Year 0	-$300,000	-$300,000
Year 1	+$130,000	+$116,071
Year 2	+$130,000	+$103,635
Year 3	+$130,000	+$92,531
		+$12,237

* The present value has been calculated using the formula

$$\text{Present value} = \frac{\text{Future cash flow}}{(1 + 0.12)^{\text{Number of years}}}$$

Using the discounted cash flow formula, we have established the following:

* **$130,000 in one year's time is worth $116,071 in today's terms**
* **$130,000 in two years' time is worth $103,635 in today's terms**
* **$130,000 in three years' time is worth $92,531 in today's terms**

Adding up these three net cash inflows gives us $312,237. This is clearly greater than the proposed initial outlay of $300,000. The net present value of the project is established by adding up all the future net cash flows (converted into today's terms) and deducting the original amount invested. In this instance, we get a net present value of $12,237.

What does this tell us? It is definitely not the profit of the project; we have already established that is $90,000. Also, it cannot be what $90,000 profit in three years' time is worth today; it must be worth more than $12,237. What it is telling us is that if we invested $300,000 in this project, we would end up being $12,237 better off in today's terms than if we invested the money in another project earning 12% per annum. This enables us to decide whether or not to proceed.

If the net present value is positive, it is saying: 'Choose me – I am better than your next best alternative.' However, if it is negative, it is saying: 'Turn me down – I cannot beat your next best alternative.'

You should note that when using net present value, unlike when dealing with return on investment and payback, no explicit comparison is needed against competing projects or predetermined targets. Such comparisons have already been built into the calculations by utilizing a required rate of return to discount future cash flows.

The bare bones
Net present value converts all future cash flows into today's terms in order to determine whether or not a long-term project is commercially viable.

There are arguments for and against this particular technique. On the positive side, it is argued that net present value is the most powerful of all the techniques commonly used to evaluate long-term projects, since it accounts for the three commercial issues that affect performance:

* **Profit**
* **Cash flow**
* **Time value of money (i.e. recognizing that cash in the future is not the same as cash now)**

Against this must be balanced certain drawbacks:

* It is conceptually difficult for many people to understand
* It relies on accurate forecasting regarding the timing and value of cash flows
* It is very sensitive to the rate of return used to discount future cash flows (a small change in the assumed rate of return might reverse a decision)

When dealing with projects that may last only two or three years, the time value of money is not always that relevant. With such projects return on investment and/or payback are often viewed as more appropriate. Net present value tends to be employed for longer-term projects that span several years.

What is internal rate of return?

'Internal rate of return' (or IRR) builds on the principles of net present value. If you understand net present value, you are most of the way to understanding internal rate of return. The objective of net present value is to assign a monetary benefit to a project that allows for when cash moves in and out of the business. Internal rate of return assigns a percentage rate of return rather than a monetary benefit, but it is a rate that (like net present value) allows for when cash moves in and moves out.

You are no doubt wondering how internal rate of return is calculated. Unfortunately, the mathematics is involved and normally demands the use of a spreadsheet. Despite this, a reasonable internal rate of return can be identified using a technique handed down through the ages known as guesswork! Let's return to Sparky Electronics' cost–benefit analysis for the final time.

When we calculated the net present value of this project, we noted that the company wanted a minimum rate of return of 12% per annum. We also noted the project had a positive value of $12,237. For this to be the case, it follows that the rate of return being earned on funds invested must be greater than the minimum required rate of 12% per annum. If the net present value had been negative, the rate of return would have had to be lower than 12%. As a result, the 'internal

	YEAR 0	YEAR 1	YEAR 2	YEAR 3	TOTAL
	$	$	$	$	$
BENEFITS					
Additional sales		500,000	500,000	500,000	1,500,000
COSTS					
Equipment	–300,000				–300,000
Cost of sales		–320,000	–320,000	–320,000	–960,000
Operating costs		–50,000	–50,000	–50,000	–150,000
NET CASH FLOW	–300,000	130,000	130,000	130,000	90,000

COST–BENEFIT ANALYSIS – REVISITED

rate of return' being achieved must be equivalent to the rate of return that, when used in net present value calculations, would yield a net present value of zero. This is because, if a project yields a net present value of zero, we are being told that the rate of return being achieved is the same as the hurdle rate.

In the case of Sparky Electronics, given the positive net present value, we know that the project must be earning more than 12%. By means of a spreadsheet – or by successive guesses – you can determine that the internal rate of return works out at approximately 14.4%.

The bare bones
Internal rate of return describes the rate of return earned on a project allowing for when cash flows take place.

This may appear to be a very complex method for working out a humble percentage. Indeed, you may be wondering what the difference is between the return on investment method examined earlier in this chapter and the internal rate of return method being discussed here. When we calculated the return on investment based on the figures in the above cost–benefit analysis, we found it to be 20%. This is in stark contrast to the internal rate of return we have just estimated of 14.4%. Why the difference?

Return on investment is calculated using the total net cash inflow achieved over the three years – whether it is mainly earned in the first year or the last year is not deemed relevant. Internal rate of return, by contrast, needs to know the net cash inflow for each year. If the $1,500,000 total sales in the above cost–benefit analysis all took place in the third year, the profit of the project would still be $90,000 and the return on investment would remain at 20%. However, the internal rate of return would fall below 14.4%, because this technique says that $500,000 per annum for three years is more valuable than $1,500,000 in the third year.

As with return on investment and payback, there are two ways in which the accept or reject decision can be made using internal rate of return. When looking at competing projects, the business might decide to proceed with the project delivering the highest internal rate of return. Alternatively, the business may establish a hurdle rate at the start of the year. If the internal rate of return is above this, it would suggest that the project should proceed. Conversely, if the internal rate of return is below the hurdle rate, it should be rejected.

Internal rate of return tends to be applied to projects where the time value of money is regarded as significant. This means that, as with net present value, it is typically applied to projects that span several years.

Stripping it down to basics...

To decide whether to accept or reject a long-term project, consideration must be given to the opportunity cost of making the decision. Four techniques are commonly used to evaluate opportunity cost: return on investment, payback, net present value, and internal rate of return. Return on investment examines the rate of return being achieved on funds invested and tends to be used by businesses that are concerned about reported profits. Payback identifies how long it takes for a project to pay for itself and tends to be used by businesses that are concerned about cash flow. Net present value examines the value of a project allowing for when cash will move in and out of the business. Internal rate of return provides a rate of return on funds invested but, unlike return on investment, it allows for when cash will move in and out of the business. Both net present value and internal rate of return tend to be used by businesses when dealing with projects that span several years.

Part Four

SUMMARY

To manage the finances of a business

you need to know where you are going,

you need to understand the information around you,

and you need to control where you are going

18 HOW DO THE PIECES FIT TOGETHER?

Over the previous 17 chapters, we have covered all the financial concepts you need as a manager. However, it is one thing to understand the principles – it is a very different matter to appreciate how they all interrelate.

This is a short but important chapter that does not introduce any new technical skills. **In this chapter we are going to examine how the various issues covered throughout this book can be brought together to help you manage a profitable business.**

How do you manage a profitable business?

We have noted that making profit involves three stages:

* **Raising funds to finance assets**
* **Turning assets into sales**
* **Turning sales into profit**

Given that the ability to turn sales into profit is contingent on cost management, the profit-making process can be seen as comprising five core elements:

* **Funds**
* **Assets**

* **Sales**
* **Costs**
* **Profit**

Managing a profitable business is all about juggling these elements to ensure a healthy profit. Consequently, running a profitable business involves applying several disciplines on an ongoing basis. Simply concentrating on one or two issues while neglecting others can rapidly lead to business failure.

FINANCIAL MANAGEMENT IS A JUGGLING ACT

What we have been looking at in this book is the financial machine – a machine that combines funds, assets, sales, and costs to generate profit. In Chapter 1 we noted that in order to study its operation, there will be a starting point, a journey, and a destination. Building on this, the diagram overleaf reviews what we covered in the preceding chapters.

We are now in a position to develop a structured approach to managing a profitable business, and that is outlined on the next few pages. Asking the questions indicated on a regular basis will highlight when and where management action is required. Vigilance is key to sound financial management.

The point to remember is that all businesses involve an element of risk. It is regrettable that some fail simply because they have a piece of bad luck that is totally outside their control, for example their premises may be destroyed by a flood. No amount of financial discipline will change the weather! Fortunately, this is the exception rather than the rule. By adhering to the concepts detailed in this book, you can considerably reduce the risk of any business failing.

THE STARTING POINT

Where do you want to go?

SETTING FINANCIAL OBJECTIVES
Chapters 2 and 3 explain how **funds**
invested in a business are turned into
profit
Chapters 4 and 5 explain the key
measures used to monitor the
performance of **funds**, **assets**, **sales**,
costs and **profit**

THE JOURNEY

How are you progressing?

USING FINANCIAL INFORMATION
Chapters 6 and 7 explain how financial
statements can be used to assess how
effectively **funds**, **assets**, **sales** and
costs have been combined to generate
profit in the past
Chapters 8 and 9 explain how share price
information can be used to assess the
ability of management to turn **funds** into
profit in the future

THE DESTINATION

Are you going in the right
direction?

PROVIDING FINANCIAL CONTROL
Chapter 10 explains how to create a
coherent plan combining **funds**, **assets**,
sales and **costs** to generate **profit**
Chapters 11, 12 and 13 explain how to
balance **sales** and **costs** in order to
achieve **profit**
Chapters 14 and 15 explain how to
manage short-term **assets**
Chapters 16 and 17 explain how to
manage long-term **assets**

MANAGING THE FINANCIAL MACHINE

SKILL SET	RELEVANT CHAPTERS	REQUIRED ACTION
SETTING FINANCIAL OBJECTIVES demands the ability to do two things		
Understand the role of profit	2 and 3	Keep focused on the profit objective. Review each business activity by asking a question: • How is this activity going to help generate **profit**?
Monitor the key measures of financial performance	4 and 5	Evaluate all five elements of the profit-making process (funds, assets, sales, costs and profit). This requires asking five questions: • Are the levels and types of **funding** appropriate to the level of business? • Are **assets** being utilized effectively? • Are there any actions that can be taken to enhance **sales**? • Is there any way **costs** can be managed more effectively? • Is the level of **profit** being achieved adequate?

SKILL SET	RELEVANT CHAPTERS	REQUIRED ACTION
USING FINANCIAL INFORMATION demands the ability to do two things		
Analyze financial statements	6 and 7	Review financial statements to assess performance and ask a question: • Are we happy with past **profit** performance?
Analyze share price information	8 and 9	Review share price information on a regular basis to assess competitors and the state of the sector and ask a question: • What can we expect in terms of future **profit** performance?
PROVIDING FINANCIAL CONTROL demands the ability to do three things		
Create sound financial plans	10	Combine all financial aspects of a business in a plan by asking a question: • How can **funds**, **assets**, **sales** and **costs** be combined to generate healthy **profit** in the future?

Manage sales and costs to ensure the attainment of profit	11, 12 and 13	Continually balance costs and sales to ensure profit is generated. This requires two questions to be asked: • Are planned **sales** being achieved? • Are **costs** appropriate to the current level of sales?
Manage assets to generate sales	14, 15, 16 and 17	Given that assets directly affect funding requirements, two questions need to be asked: • Are net current **assets** appropriate to the level of business? Are fixed **assets** appropriate to the level of business?

A parting thought

In this text we have covered all the tools you need to make sound, financially based business decisions. Don't let people tell you 'Our business is far more complicated than that!' or 'We're different!' No matter what business you look at, it can be broken down into five elements: there will be funding, there will be assets, there will be sales, there will be costs, and there will be profit (or loss!). Consequently, the issues we have examined in the preceding chapters apply to every business. The fastest way to resolve many business challenges is to strip them back to basics and determine whether or not financial principles are being successfully applied.

Index